A Return
to Love

A Return to Love

Reflections on the Principles of
A COURSE IN MIRACLES

Marianne Williamson

"Be not afraid, but let your world be lit by miracles."

—A Course in Miracles

HarperOne
An Imprint of HarperCollinsPublishers

Kind acknowledgment is made for permission to reprint the following:
Portions reprinted by permission from *A Course in Miracles*. Copyright ©
1975, Foundation for Inner Peace, Inc. All chapter headings and sub-
chapter headings are taken from *A Course in Miracles*.
Excerpts from *Quantum Healing* by Deepak Chopra. Copyright © 1989.
Reprinted by permission of Bantam Books, a division of Bantam, Double-
day, Dell Publishing Group.
The quotation from "The Song of Prayer" which is on p. 267 is used by
permission of the copyright owner, The Foundation for Inner Peace, P.O.
Box 1104, Glen Ellen, CA 95442.
Any quoted unattributed material comes from *A Course in Miracles*.

HarperCollins books may be purchased for educational, business, or
sales promotional use. For information please e-mail the Special Markets
Department at SPsales@harpercollins.com.

First HarperPerennial edition published 1993. Reissued in 1996.

FIRST HARPERONE EDITION PUBLISHED 2012

The Library of Congress has catalogued the hardcover edition of this book
as follows:

Williamson, Marienne.
    A return to love : reflections on the principles of A course in miracles
/ Marianne Williamson. — 1st ed.
    p. cm.
    ISBN 978-0-06-092748-6
    1. Course in miracles. 2. New Age movement. 3 Spiritual life.
I. Title.
BP605.N48W56   1992
299'.93—dc20   91–55511

21 22 23 24 LSC(H) 80 79 78 77

For both my fathers,
who art in Heaven.

CONTENTS

ACKNOWLEDGMENTS

This new edition of *A Return to Love* is possible because of the book's popularity since 1992. For that, my deepest thanks to Oprah Winfrey. Her enthusiasm and generosity have given the book, and me, an audience we would never otherwise have had.

Many thanks as well to my literary agent, Al Lowman. Because of him I started the book, and because of him I finished it. Andrea Cagan also did much to help bring this book to completion. Her contribution was enormous. Thanks to Carol Cohen, Adrian Zackheim, Mitchell Ivers, and all the others at HarperCollins who helped produce this new edition. For my friends Rich Cooper, Norma Ferarra, Bruce Bierman, Tara Shannon, David Kessler, and Victoria Pearman, my gratitude is deep and abiding.

Thanks to every person who has attended my lectures since I began giving them.

Thanks to my parents for all they've given me, and to my daughter for bringing a sweetness to my life that soars way beyond words.

And most of all, thanks to all the many people who have read *A Return to Love* since it was first published and shared with me such powerful testimony of its value to their lives. Their support for my efforts means more to me than I can express on this page.

PREFACE

I grew up in a middle-class Jewish family, laced with the magical overtones of an eccentric father. When I was thirteen, in 1965, he took me to Saigon to show me what war was. The Vietnam War was beginning to rev up and he wanted me to see bullet holes firsthand. He didn't want the military-industrial complex to eat my brain and convince me war was okay.

My grandfather was very religious and sometimes I would go to synagogue with him on Saturday mornings. When the ark was opened during the service, he would bow and begin to cry. I would cry too, but I don't know whether I was crying out of a budding religious fervor, or simply because he was.

When I went to high school, I took my first philosophy class and decided God was a crutch I didn't need. What kind of God would let children starve, I argued, or people get cancer, or the Holocaust happen? The innocent faith of a child met the pseudointellectualism of a high school sophomore head on. I wrote a Dear John letter to God. I was depressed as I wrote it, but it was something I felt I had to do because I was too well-read now to believe in God.

During college, a lot of what I learned from professors was definitely extra-curricular. I left school to grow vegetables, but I don't remember ever growing any. There are a lot of things from those years I can't remember. Like a lot of people at that time—late sixties, early seventies—I was pretty wild. Every door marked "no" by conventional standards seemed to hold the key to some lascivious pleasure I had to have. Whatever sounded outrageous, I wanted to do. And usually, I did.

I didn't know what to do with my life, though I remember my parents kept begging me to do *something*. I went from relationship to relationship, job to job, city to city, looking for some sense of identity or purpose, some feeling that my life had finally kicked in. I knew I had talent, but I didn't know at what. I knew I had intelligence, but I was too frantic to apply it to my own circumstances. I went into therapy several times, but it rarely made an impact. I sank deeper and deeper into my own neurotic patterns, seeking relief in food, drugs, people, or whatever else I could find to distract me from myself. I was always trying to make something happen in my life, but nothing much happened except all the drama I created around things not happening.

There was some huge rock of self-loathing sitting in the middle of my stomach during those years, and it got worse with every phase I went through. As my pain deepened, so did my interest in philosophy: Eastern, Western, academic, esoteric. Kierkegaard, the I Ching, existentialism, radical death-of-God Christian theology, Buddhism, and more. I always sensed there was some mysterious cosmic order to things, but I could never figure out how it applied to my own life.

One day I was sitting around smoking marijuana with my brother, and he told me that everybody thought I was weird. "It's like you have some kind of virus," he said. I remember thinking I was going to shoot out of my body in that moment. I felt like an alien. I had often felt as though life was a private club and everybody had received the password except me. Now was one of those times. I felt other people knew a secret that I didn't know, but I didn't want to ask them about it because I didn't want them to know I didn't know.

By my mid-twenties, I was a total mess.

I believed other people were dying inside too, just like me, but they couldn't or wouldn't talk about it. I kept thinking there was something very important that no one was discussing. I didn't have the words myself, but I was sure that something was fundamentally off in the world. How could everybody think that this stupid game of "making it in the world"—which I was actually embarrassed I didn't know how to play—could be all there is to our being here?

One day in 1977, I saw a set of blue books with gold lettering sitting on someone's coffee table in New York City. I opened to the introduction. It read,

> "This is A Course in Miracles. *It is a required course. Only the time you take it is voluntary. Free will does not mean that you can establish the curriculum. It means only that you can elect what you want to take at a given time. The Course does not aim at teaching the meaning of love, for that is beyond what can be taught. It does aim, however, at removing the blocks to the awareness of love's presence, which is your natural inheritance.*"

I remember thinking that sounded rather intriguing, if not arrogant. Reading further, however, I noticed Christian terminology throughout the books. This made me nervous. Although I had studied Christian theology in school, I had kept it at an intellectual distance. Now I felt the threat of a more personal significance. I put the books back on the table.

It took another year before I picked them up again— another year, and another year's misery. Then I was ready.

This time I was so depressed I didn't even notice the language. This time, I knew immediately that the Course had something very important to teach me. It used traditional Christian terms, but in decidedly nontraditional, nonreligious ways. I was struck, as most people are, by the profound authority of its voice. It answered questions I had begun to think were unanswerable. It talked about God in brilliant psychological terms, challenging my intelligence and never insulting it. It's a bit cliché to say this, but I felt like I had come home.

The Course seemed to have a basic message: *relax*. I was confused to hear that because I had always associated relaxing with resigning. I had been waiting for someone to explain to me how to fight the fight, or to fight the fight for me, and now this book suggested that I surrender the fight completely. I was surprised but so relieved. I had long suspected I wasn't made for worldly combat.

For me, this was not just another book. This was my personal teacher, my path out of hell. As I began reading the Course and following its Workbook exercises, I could feel almost immediately that the changes it produced inside of me were positive. I felt happy. I felt like I was beginning to calm down. I began to understand myself, to get some hook on why my relationships had been so painful, why I could never stay with anything, why I hated my body. Most importantly, I began to have some sense that I could change. Studying the Course unleashed huge amounts of hopeful energy inside me, energy that had been turning darker and more self-destructive every day.

The Course, a self-study program of spiritual psycho-therapy contained in three books, claims no monopoly on God. It is a statement of universal spiritual themes. There's only one truth, spoken different ways, and the Course is just one path to it out of many. If it's your path, however, you know it. For me, the Course was a breakthrough experience intellectually, emotionally, and psychologically. It freed me from a terrible emotional pain.

I wanted that "awareness of love's presence" that I had read about, and over the next five years I studied the Course passionately. As my mother said at the time, I "read it like a menu." In 1983, I began sharing my understanding of the Course with a small gathering of people in Los Angeles. The group began to grow. Since then, my lecture audiences have grown significantly here and abroad. I have had the opportunity to see how relevant this material is to people throughout the world.

A Return to Love is based on what I have learned from *A Course in Miracles.* It is about some of the Course's basic principles as I understand them and relate them to various issues that affect our daily lives.

A Return to Love is about the practice of love, as a strength and not a weakness, as a daily answer to the problems that confront us. How is love a practical solution? This book is written as a guide to the miraculous application of love as a balm on every wound. Whether our psychic pain is in the area of relationships, health, career, or elsewhere, love is a potent force, the cure, the Answer.

Americans are not that big on philosophy. We're very big on action, however, once we understand the reason for it. As we begin to understand more deeply why love is such a necessary element in the healing of the world, a shift will occur in how we live our lives within and without.

My prayer is that this book might help someone. I have written it with an open heart. I hope you'll read it with an open mind.

Marianne Williamson
Los Angeles, CA

INTRODUCTION

When we were born, we were programmed perfectly. We had a natural tendency to focus on love. Our imaginations were creative and flourishing, and we knew how to use them. We were connected to a world much richer than the one we connect to now, a world full of enchantment and a sense of the miraculous.

So what happened? Why is it that we reached a certain age, looked around, and the enchantment was gone?

Because we were taught to focus elsewhere. We were taught to think unnaturally. We were taught a very bad philosophy, a way of looking at the world that contradicts who we are.

We were taught to think thoughts like competition, struggle, sickness, finite resources, limitation, guilt, bad, death, scarcity, and loss. We began to think these things, and so we began to know them. We were taught that things like grades, being good enough, money, and doing things the right way, are more important than love. We were taught that we're separate from other people, that we have to compete to get ahead, that we're not quite good enough the way we are. We were taught to see the world the way that others had come to see it. It's as though, as soon as we got here, we were given a sleeping pill. The thinking of the world, which is not based on love, began pounding in our ears the moment we hit shore.

Love is what we were born with. Fear is what we have learned here. The spiritual journey is the relinquishment—or unlearning—of fear and the acceptance of love back into our hearts. Love is the essential existential fact. It is our ultimate reality and our purpose on earth. To be consciously aware of it, to experience love in ourselves and others, is the meaning of life.

Meaning doesn't lie in things. Meaning lies in us. When we attach value to things that aren't love—the money, the car, the house, the prestige—we are loving things that can't love us back. We are searching for meaning in the meaningless. Money, of itself, means nothing. Material things, of themselves, mean nothing. It's not that they're bad. It's that they're nothing.

We came here to co-create with God by extending love. Life spent with any other purpose in mind is meaningless, contrary to our nature, and ultimately painful. It's as though we've been lost in a dark, parallel universe where things are loved more than people. We overvalue what we perceive with our physical senses, and undervalue what we know to be true in our hearts.

Love isn't seen with the physical eyes or heard with physical ears. The physical senses can't perceive it; it's perceived through another kind of vision. Metaphysicians call it the Third Eye, esoteric Christians call it the vision of the Holy Spirit, and others call it the Higher Self. Regardless of what it's called, love requires a different kind of "seeing" than we're used to—a different kind of knowing or thinking. Love is the intuitive knowledge of our hearts. It's a "world beyond" that we all secretly long for. An ancient memory of this love haunts all of us all the time, and beckons us to return.

Love isn't material. It's energy. It's the feeling in a room, a situation, a person. Money can't buy it. Sex doesn't guarantee it. It has nothing at all to do with the physical world, but it can be expressed nonetheless. We experience it as kindness, giving, mercy, compassion, peace, joy, acceptance, non-judgment, joining, and intimacy.

Fear is our shared lovelessness, our individual and collective hells. It's a world that seems to press on us from within and without, giving constant false testimony to the meaninglessness of love. When fear is expressed, we recognize it as anger, abuse, disease, pain, greed, addiction, selfishness, obsession, corruption, violence, and war.

Love is within us. It cannot be destroyed, but can only be hidden. The world we knew as children is still buried within our minds. I once read a delightful book called *The Mists of Avalon*. The mists of Avalon are a mythical allusion to the tales of King Arthur. Avalon is a magical island that is hidden behind huge impenetrable mists. Unless the mists part, there is no way to navigate your way to the island. But unless you believe the island is there, the mists won't part.

Avalon symbolizes a world beyond the world we see with our physical eyes. It represents a miraculous sense of things, the enchanted realm that we knew as children. Our childlike self is the deepest level of our being. It is who we really are and what is real doesn't go away. The truth doesn't stop being the truth just because we're not looking at it. Love merely becomes clouded over, or surrounded by mental mists.

Avalon is the world we knew when we were still connected to our softness, our innocence, our spirit. It's actually the same world we see now, but informed by love, interpreted gently, with hope and faith and a sense of wonder. It's easily retrieved, because perception is a choice. The mists part when we believe that Avalon is behind them.

And that's what a miracle is: a parting of the mists, a shift in perception, a return to love.

A Return
to Love

PART I

Principles

CHAPTER 1

Hell

"There is no place for hell in a world whose loveliness can yet be so intense and so inclusive it is but a step from there to Heaven."

1. THE DARKNESS

> *"The journey into darkness has been long and cruel, and you have gone deep into it."*

Many of us know in our hearts that we never really grew up. The problem isn't that we're lost or apathetic, narcissistic or materialistic. The problem is we're terrified.

A lot of us know we have what it takes—the looks, the education, the talent, the credentials. But in certain areas, we're paralyzed. We're not being stopped by something on the outside, but by something on the inside. Our oppression is internal. The government isn't holding us back, or hunger or poverty. We're not afraid we'll get sent to Siberia. We're just afraid, period. Our fear is free-floating. We're afraid this isn't the right relationship or we're afraid it is. We're afraid they won't like us or we're afraid they will. We're afraid of failure or we're afraid of success. We're afraid of dying young or we're afraid of growing old. We're more afraid of life than we are of death.

You'd think we'd have some compassion for ourselves, bound up in emotional chains the way we are, but we don't. We're just disgusted with ourselves, because we think we should be better by now. Sometimes we make the mistake of thinking other people don't have as much fear as we do, which only makes us more afraid. Maybe they know something we don't know. Maybe we're missing a chromosome.

It's become popular these days to blame practically everything on our parents. We figure it's because of them that our self-esteem is so low. If only they'd been different, we'd be brimming with self-love. But if you take a close look at how our parents treated us, whatever abuse they gave us was often mild compared to the way we abuse ourselves today. It's true that your mother might have said repeatedly, "You'll never be able to do that, dear." But now you say to yourself, "You're a jerk. You never do it right. You blew it. I hate you." They might have been mean, but we're vicious.

Many of us have slipped into a barely camouflaged vortex of self-loathing. And we're always, even desperately, seeking a way out, through growth or through escape. Maybe this degree will do it, or this job, this seminar, this therapist, this relationship, this diet, or this project. But too often the medicine falls short of a cure, and the chains just keep getting thicker and tighter. The same soap operas develop with different people in different cities. We begin to realize that we ourselves are somehow the problem, but we don't know what to do about it. We're not powerful enough to overrule ourselves. We sabotage, abort everything: our careers, our relationships, even our children. We drink. We do drugs. We control. We obsess. We codepend. We overeat. We hide. We attack. The form of the dysfunction is irrelevant. We can find a lot of different ways to express how much we hate ourselves.

But express it we will. Emotional energy has got to go somewhere, and self-loathing is a powerful emotion. Turned inward, it becomes our personal hells: addiction, obsession, compulsion, depression, violent relationships, illness. Projected outward, it becomes our collective hells: violence, war, crime, oppression. But it's all the same thing: hell has many mansions, too.

I remember, years ago, having an image in my mind that frightened me terribly. I would see a sweet, innocent little girl in a perfect white organdy apron, pinned screaming with her back against a wall. A vicious, hysterical woman was repeatedly stabbing her through the heart with a knife. I suspected that both characters were me, that they lived as psychic forces inside my mind. With every passing year, I grew more scared of that woman with the knife. She was active in my system. She was totally out of control, and I felt like she wanted to kill me.

When I was most desperate, I looked for a lot of ways out of my personal hell. I read books about how our minds create our experience, how the brain is like a bio-computer that manufactures whatever we feed into it with our thoughts. "Think success and you'll get it," "Expect to fail and you will," I read. But no matter how much I worked at changing my thoughts, I kept going back to the painful ones. Temporary breakthroughs would occur: I would work on having a more positive attitude, get myself together and meet a new man or get a new job. But I would always revert to the patterns of self-betrayal: I'd eventually turn into a bitch with the man, or screw up at the job. I would lose ten pounds, and then put them back on in five minutes, terrified by how it felt to look beautiful. The only thing more frightening than not getting male attention, was getting lots of it. The groove of sabotage ran deep and automatic. Sure, I could change my thoughts, but not permanently. And there's only one despair worse than "God, I blew it."—and that's, "God, I blew it *again.*"

My painful thoughts were my demons. Demons are insidious. Through various therapeutic techniques, I'd become very smart about my own neuroses, but that didn't necessarily exorcise them. The garbage didn't go away; it just became more sophisticated. I used to tell a person what my weaknesses were, using such conscious language that they would think, "Well, obviously she knows what her patterns are, so she won't do *that* again."

But oh yes, I would. Acknowledging my patterns was just a way of diverting someone's attention. Then

I'd go into a rampage or other outrageous behavior so quickly and smoothly that no one, least of all myself, could do anything to stop me before I'd ruined a situation completely. I would say the exact words that would make the man leave, or make someone fire me, or worse. In those days, it never occurred to me to ask for a miracle.

For one thing, I wouldn't have known what a miracle was. I put them in the pseudo-mystical-religious garbage category. I didn't know, until reading *A Course in Miracles*, that a miracle is a reasonable thing to ask for. I didn't know that a miracle is just a shift in perception.

I once attended a twelve-step meeting where people were asking God to take away their desire to drink. I had never gone overboard with any one particular dysfunctional behavior. It wasn't drinking or drugs that was doing me in; it was my personality in general, that hysterical woman inside my head. My negativity was as destructive to me as alcohol is to the alcoholic. I was an artist at finding my own jugular. It was as though I was addicted to my own pain. Could I ask God to help me with that? It occurred to me that, just as with any other addictive behavior, maybe a power greater than myself could turn things around. Neither my intellect nor my willpower had been able to do that. Understanding what occurred when I was three years old hadn't been enough to free me. Problems I kept thinking would eventually go away, kept getting worse every year. I hadn't emotionally developed the way I should have, and I knew it. Somehow, somewhere, it was as though wires deep inside my brain had gotten crossed. Like a lot of other people in my generation and culture, I had gotten off track many years before, and in certain ways just never grew up. We've had the longest postadolescence in the history of the world. Like emotional stroke victims, we need to go back a few steps in order to go forward. We need someone to teach us the basics.

For me, no matter what hot water I had gotten into, I had always thought that I could get myself out of it. I was cute enough, or smart enough, or talented enough, or clever enough—and if nothing else worked, I could call my father and ask for money. But finally I got myself into so much trouble, that I knew I needed more help than I could muster up myself. At twelve-step meetings, I kept hearing it said that a power greater than I could do for me what I couldn't do for myself. There was nothing else to do and there was no one left to call. My fear finally became so great, that I wasn't too hip to say "God, please help me."

2. *THE LIGHT*

"The light is in you."

So I went through this grandiose, dramatic moment where I invited God into my life. It was terrifying at first, but then I kind of got off on the idea.

After that, nothing really felt the way I expected it to.

I had thought that things would improve. It's as though my life was a house, and I thought God would give it a wonderful paint job—new shutters perhaps, a pretty portico, new roof. Instead, it felt as though, as soon as I gave the house to God, He hit it with a giant wrecking ball. "Sorry, honey," He seemed to say, "There were cracks in the foundation, not to mention all the rats in the bedroom. I thought we better just start all over."

I had read about people surrendering to God and then feeling this profound sense of peace descend like a mantle over their shoulders. I did get that feeling, but only for about a minute and a half. After that, I just felt like I'd been busted. This didn't turn me off to God so much as it made me respect His intelligence. It implied He understood the situation better than I would have expected. If I was God, I'd have busted me too. I felt more grateful than resentful. I was desperate for help.

A certain amount of desperation is usually necessary before we're ready for God. When it came to spiritual surrender, I didn't get serious, not really, until I was down on my knees completely. The mess got so thick that all the king's horses and all the king's men couldn't make Marianne function again. The hysterical woman inside me was in a maniacal rage, and the innocent child was pinned to the wall. I fell apart. I crossed the line between in-pain-but-still-able-to-function-normally, and the realm of the total basket case. I had what is commonly called a nervous breakdown.

Nervous breakdowns can be highly underrated methods of spiritual transformation. They certainly get your attention. I have seen people have little minibreakdowns year after year, each time stopping just short of getting the point. I think I was lucky to get mine over with in one fell swoop. The things I learned here, I will not forget. As painful as this experience was, I now see it as an important, perhaps necessary step in my breakthrough to a happier life.

For one thing, I was profoundly humbled. I saw very clearly that, of myself, I am nothing. Until this happens, you keep trying all your old tricks, the ones that never did work but that you keep thinking might work this time. Once you've had enough and you can't do it anymore, you consider the possibility that there might be a better way. That's when your head cracks open and God comes in.

I felt during those years as though my skull had exploded. It seemed as though thousands of little pieces of it had shot into outer space. Very slowly, they began to come together again. But while my emotional brain was so exposed, it seemed to be rewired, like I'd had some kind of psychic surgery. I felt like I became a different person.

More people have felt their heads crack open in some way, than have admitted it to their friends. These days it's not an uncommon phenomenon. People are crashing into walls today—socially, biologically, psychologically and emotionally. But this isn't bad news. In a way, it's good. Until your knees finally hit the floor, you're just playing at life, and on some level you're scared because you know you're just playing. The moment of surrender is not when life is over. It's when it begins.

Not that that moment of eureka—that calling out to God—is it, and it's all Paradise from then on. You've simply started the climb. But you know you're not running around in circles at the bottom of the mountain anymore, never really getting anywhere, dreaming of the top and having no idea how to get there. For many people, things have to get very bad before there's a shift. When you truly bottom out, there comes an exhilarating release. You recognize there's a power in the universe bigger than you are, who can do for you what you can't do for yourself. All of a sudden, your last resort sounds like a very good idea.

How ironic. You spend your whole life resisting the notion that there's someone out there smarter than you are, and then all of a sudden you're so relieved to know it's true. All of a sudden, you're not too proud to ask for help.

That's what it means to surrender to God.

CHAPTER 2

God

"You are in God."

1.   GOD IS THE ROCK

"There is no time, no place, no state where God is absent."

There have been times in my life—and they still happen today, though they're more the exception now than the rule—when I have felt as though sadness would overwhelm me. Something didn't turn out the way I wanted it to, or I was in conflict with someone, or I was afraid of what might or might not happen in the future. Life in those moments can be difficult to bear, and the mind begins an endless search for its escape from pain.

What I learned from *A Course in Miracles* is that the change we're really looking for is inside our heads. Events are always in flux. One day people love you; the next day you're their target. One day a situation is running smoothly; the next day chaos reigns. One day you feel like you're an okay person; the next day you feel like you're an utter failure. These changes in life are always going to happen; they're part of the human experience.

What we can change, however, is how we perceive them. And that shift in our perception is a miracle.

There's a biblical story where Jesus says we can build our house on sand or we can build it on rock. Our house is our emotional stability. When it is built on sand, then the winds and rain can tear it down. One disappointing phone call and we crumble; one storm and the house falls down.

When our house is built on rock, then it is sturdy and strong and the storms can't destroy it. We are not so vulnerable to life's passing dramas. Our stability rests on something more enduring than the current weather, something permanent and strong. We're depending on God.

I had never realized that depending on God meant depending on love. I had heard it said that God was love, but it had never kicked in for me exactly what that meant.

As I began to study *A Course in Miracles*, I discovered the following things:

> *God is the love within us.*

> *Whether we "follow Him," or think with love, is entirely up to us.*

> *When we choose to love, or to allow our minds to be one with God, then life is peaceful. When we turn away from love, the pain sets in.*

And whether we love, or close our hearts to love, is a mental choice we make, every moment of every day.

2.   *LOVE IS GOD*

> *"Love does not conquer all things, but it does set all things right."*

Love taken seriously is a radical outlook, a major departure from the psychological orientation that rules the world. It is threatening not because it is a small idea, but because it is so huge.

For many people, God is a frightening concept. Asking God for help doesn't seem very comforting if we think of Him as something outside ourselves, or capricious or judgmental. But God is love. We were created in His image, or mind, which means that we are extensions of His love. This is why we are called the Sons of God.

We think we authored God, rather than realizing that He authored us. The Course says we have an authority problem. Rather than accepting that we are the loving beings that He created, we have arrogantly thought that we could create ourselves, and then create God. Because *we* are angry and judgmental, we have projected those characteristics onto Him. We have made up a God in *our* image. But God remains who He is and always has been: the energy, the thought of unconditional love. He cannot think with anger or judgment; He is mercy and compassion and total acceptance. The problem is that we have forgotten this, and so we have forgotten who we ourselves are.

I began to realize that taking love seriously would be a complete transformation of my thinking. *A Course in Miracles* calls itself a mind training in the relinquishment of a thought system based on fear, and the acceptance instead of a thought system based on love. Now, over a decade since starting the study of *A Course in Miracles*, my mind is hardly the touchstone of holy perception. I certainly don't pretend to consistently achieve a loving perspective of every situation in my own life. One thing I'm very clear about, however, is that when I do, life works beautifully. And when I don't, things stay stuck.

In order to love purely, we must surrender our old ways of thinking. For most of us, surrendering anything is difficult. We still think of surrender as failure, as something you do when you've lost the war. But spiritual surrender, although passive, is not weak. Actually, it is strong. It is a balance to our aggression. Although aggression is not bad—it is at the heart of creativity—it needs to be tempered by love in order to be an agent of harmony rather than violence. The mind that's separate from God has forgotten how to check in with love before it saunters out into the world. Without love, our actions are hysterical. Without love, we have no wisdom.

To surrender to God means to let go and just love. By affirming that love is our priority in a situation, we actualize the power of God. This is not metaphor; it's fact. We literally use our minds to co-create with Him. Through a mental decision—a conscious recognition of love's importance and our willingness to experience it— we "call on a higher power." We set aside our normal mental habit patterns and allow them to be superseded by a different, gentler mode of perception. That is what it means to let a power greater than we are direct our lives.

Once we get to the point where we realize that God is love, we understand that following God simply means following the dictates of love. The hurdle we have to face next is the question of whether or not love is such a wise thing to follow. The question is no longer "What is God?" The question we ask now is, "What is love?"

Love is energy. It's not something we can perceive with our physical senses, but people can usually tell you when they feel it and when they don't. Very few people feel enough love in their lives because the world has become a rather loveless place. We can hardly even imagine a world in which all of us were in love, all the time, with everyone. There would be no wars because we wouldn't fight. There would be no hunger because we would feed each other. There would be no environmental breakdown because we would love ourselves, our children and our planet too much to destroy it. There would be no prejudice, oppression or violence of any kind. There would be no sorrow. There would only be peace.

Although we may not realize it, most of us are violent people—not necessarily physically, but emotionally.

We have been brought up in a world that does not put love first, and where love is absent, fear sets in. Fear is to love as darkness is to light. It's a terrible absence of what we need in order to survive. It's a place we go where all hell breaks loose.

When infants aren't held, they can become sick, even die. It's universally accepted that children need love, but at what age are people supposed to stop needing it? We never do. We need love in order to live happily, as much as we need oxygen in order to live at all.

3.   ONLY LOVE IS REAL

"God is not the author of fear. You are."

So the problem with the world is that we have strayed from God, or wandered away from love. According to *A Course in Miracles*, this separation from God first happened millions of years ago. But the important revelation, the crux of the Course, is that in reality it never happened at all.

The introduction to *A Course in Miracles* states:

> *"The Course can be summed up very simply:*
> *Nothing real can be threatened.*
> *Nothing unreal exists.*
> *Herein lies the peace of God."*

What that means is this:

1. Love is real. It's an eternal creation and nothing can destroy it.
2. Anything that isn't love is an illusion.
3. Remember this, and you'll be at peace.

A Course in Miracles says that only love is real: "The opposite of love is fear, but what is all-encompassing can have no opposite." When we think with love, we are literally co-creating with God. And when we're not thinking with love, since only love is real, then we're actually not thinking at all. We're hallucinating. And that's what this world is: a mass hallucination, where fear seems more real than love. Fear is an illusion. Our craziness, paranoia, anxiety and trauma are literally all *imagined*. That is not to say they don't exist for us as human beings. They do. But our fear is not our ultimate reality, and it does not replace the truth of who we really are. Our love, which is our real self, doesn't die, but merely goes underground.

The Course teaches that fear is literally a bad dream. It is as though the mind has been split in two; one part stays in touch with love, and the other part veers into fear. Fear manufactures a kind of parallel universe where the unreal seems real, and the real seems unreal.

Love casts out sin or fear the way light casts out darkness. The shift from fear to love is a miracle. It doesn't fix things on the earth plane; it addresses the real source of our problems, which is always on the level of consciousness. The only real problem is a lack of love. To address the world's problems on any other level is a temporary palliative—a fix but not a healing, a treatment of the symptom but not a cure.

Thoughts are like data programmed into a computer, registered on the screen of your life. If you don't like what you see on the screen, there's no point in going up to the screen and trying to erase it. Thought is Cause; experience is Effect. If you don't like the effects in your life, you have to change the nature of your thinking.

Love in your mind produces love in your life. This is the meaning of Heaven.

Fear in your mind produces fear in your life. This is the meaning of hell.

A shift in how we think about life produces a shift in how we experience it. To say, "God, deliver me from hell," means "God, deliver me from my fearful thinking." The altar to God is the human mind. To "desecrate the altar" is to fill it with non-loving thoughts.

Adam and Eve were happy until she "ate of the knowledge of good and evil." What that means is that everything was perfect until they learned to close their hearts, to say, "I love you if you do this, but not if you do that," or, "I accept this part of you, but not that part." Closing our hearts destroys our peace because it's alien to our nature. It warps us and turns us into people we're not meant to be.

Freud defined neurosis as separation from self, and so it is. Our real self is the love within us. It's the "child of God." The fearful self is an impostor. The return to love is the great cosmic drama, the personal journey from pretense to self, from pain to inner peace.

So then it might go like this, or at least it did for me. I'd get myself into some terrible mess, and I'd remember that all I needed was a miracle, a shift in perception. I'd pray, "God, please help me. Heal my mind. Wherever my thoughts have strayed from love—if I've been controlling, manipulative, greedy, ambitious for myself—whatever it is, I'm willing to see this differently. Amen."

So, the universe would hear that, and "Ding!," I'd get my miracle. Relationship transformed, situation healed. But then I'd go back to the same kind of fearful thinking that had gotten me down on my knees to begin with, and I'd repeat the pattern. I'd get myself into some emotional car crash, once again end up on my knees, once again ask God to help me, and once again be returned to sanity and peace.

Finally, after a lot of repetition of those embattled scenarios, I said to myself, "Marianne. Next time you're down on your knees, why don't you just *stay* there?" Why don't we stay in the realm of the answer, rather than always returning to the realm of the problem? Why not seek some level of awareness where we don't *create* these problems for ourselves all the time? Let's not just ask for a new job, a new relationship, or a new body. Let's ask for a new world. Let's ask for a new life.

When I was down on my knees completely, and I knew what it meant to feel sincerely humbled, I almost expected to feel God's anger or contempt. Instead, it was as though I heard a gentle voice say, "Can we start now?" Until that point, I was hiding from my love, and so resisting my own life. The return to love is not the end of life's adventure, but the beginning. It's the return to who you really are.

CHAPTER 3

You

*"The Thought God holds of you is like a star,
unchangeable in an eternal sky."*

1. THE PERFECT YOU

"Again—nothing you do or think or wish or make is necessary to establish your worth."

You are a child of God. You were created in a blinding flash of creativity, a primal thought when God extended Himself in love. Everything you've added on since is useless.

When Michelangelo was asked how he created a piece of sculpture, he answered that the statue already existed within the marble. God Himself had created the Pietà, David, Moses. Michelangelo's job, as he saw it, was to get rid of the excess marble that surrounded God's creation.

So it is with you. The perfect you isn't something you need to create, because God already created it. The perfect you is the love within you. Your job is to allow the Holy Spirit to remove the fearful thinking that surrounds your perfect self, just as excess marble surrounded Michelangelo's perfect statue.

To remember that you are part of God, that you are loved and lovable, is not arrogant. It's humble. To think you are anything else is arrogant, because it implies you're something other than a creation of God.

Love is changeless and therefore so are you. Nothing that you have ever done or will ever do can mar your perfection in the eyes of God. You're deserving in His eyes because of what you are, not because of what you do. What you do or don't do is not what determines your essential value—your growth perhaps, but not your value. That's why God is totally approving and accepting of you, exactly as you are. What's not to like? You were not created in sin; you were created in love.

2.   THE DIVINE MIND

> *"God has lit your mind Himself, and keeps your mind lit by His Light because His Light is what your mind is."*

Psychologist Carl Jung posited the notion of the "collective unconscious," an innate mental structure encompassing the universal thought forms of all humanity. His idea was that if you went deeply enough into your mind, and deeply enough into mine, there is a level we all share. The Course goes one step further; if you go deeply enough into your mind, and deeply enough into mine, we have the *same mind*. The concept of a divine, or "Christ" mind, is the idea that, at our core, we are not just identical, but actually the same being. "There is only one begotten Son" doesn't mean that someone else was it, and we're not. It means we're all it. There's only one of us here.

We're like the spokes on a wheel, all radiating out from the same center. If you define us according to our position on the rim, we seem separate and distinct from one another. But if you define us according to our starting point, our source—the center of the wheel—we're a shared identity. If you dig deep enough into your mind, and deep enough into mine, the picture is the same: at the bottom of it all, what we are is love.

The word "Christ" is a psychological term. No religion has a monopoly on the truth. Christ refers to the common thread of divine love that is the core and essence of every human mind.

The love in one of us is the love in all of us. There's actually no place where God stops and you start, and no place where you stop and I start. Love is energy, an infinite continuum. Your mind extends into mine and into everyone else's. It doesn't stay enclosed within your body.

A Course in Miracles likens us to sunbeams thinking we're separate from the sun, or waves thinking we're separate from the ocean. Just as a sunbeam can't separate itself from the sun, and a wave can't separate itself from the ocean, we can't separate ourselves from one another. We are all part of a vast sea of love, one indivisible divine mind. This truth of who we really are doesn't change;

we just forget it. We identify with the notion of a small, separate self, instead of the idea of a reality we share with everyone.

You aren't who you think you are. Aren't you glad? You're not your grades, or your credentials, or your resumes, or your house. We aren't those things at all. We are holy beings, individual cells in the body of Christ. *A Course in Miracles* reminds us that the sun continues to shine and the ocean continues to swell, oblivious to the fact that a fraction of their identity has forgotten what it is. We are who God created us to be. We are all one, we are love itself. "Accepting the Christ" is merely a shift in self-perception. We awaken from the dream that we are finite, isolated creatures, and recognize that we are glorious, infinitely creative spirits. We awaken from the dream that we are weak, and accept that the power of the universe is within us.

I realized, many years ago, that I must be very powerful if I could mess up everything I touched, everywhere I went, with such amazing consistency. I figured there must be a way to apply the same mental power, then embedded in neurosis, in a more positive way. A lot of today's most common psychological orientation is to analyze the darkness in order to reach the light, thinking that if we focus on our neuroses—their origins and dynamics—then we will move beyond them. Eastern religions tell us that if we go for God, all that is not authentically ourselves will drop. Go for the light and darkness will disappear. Focus on Christ means focus on the goodness and power that lie latent within us, in order to invoke them into realization and expression. We get in life that which we focus on. Continual focus on darkness leads us, as individuals and as a society, further into darkness. Focus on the light brings us into the light.

"I accept the Christ within" means, "I accept the beauty within me as who I really am. I am not my weakness. I am not my anger. I am not my small-mindedness. I am much, much more. And I am willing to be reminded of who I really am."

3.   THE EGO

"The ego is quite literally a fearful thought."

As children, we were taught to be "good" boys and girls, which of course implies we were not that already. We were taught we're good if we clean up our room, or we're good if we make good grades. Very few of us were taught that we're *essentially* good. Very few of us were given a sense of unconditional approval, a feeling that we're precious because of what we *are*, not what we *do*. And that's not because we were raised by monsters. We were raised by people who were raised the same way we were. Sometimes, in fact, it was the people who loved us the most who felt it was their responsibility to train us to struggle.

Why? Because the world as it is, is tough, and they wanted us to make good. We had to become as crazy as the world is, or we would never fit in here. We had to achieve, make the grade, get into Harvard. What's strange is that we didn't learn discipline from that perspective, so much as a weird displacement of our sense of power away from ourselves and onto external sources. What we lost was a sense of our own power. And what we learned was fear, fear that we weren't good enough, just the way we are.

Fear does not promote learning. It warps us. It stunts us. It makes us neurotic. And by the time we were teenagers, most of us were severely cracked. Our love, our hearts, our real "self" were constantly invalidated by people who didn't love us and by people who did. In the absence of love, we began slowly but surely to fall apart.

Years ago, I told myself not to worry about a devil. I remember thinking that there's no force of evil out stalking the planet. That, I told myself, is all in my mind. Then I realized this is not good news. Since every thought creates experience, there's no worse place it could possibly be. While it's true there isn't an actual devil out there grabbing for our souls, there is a tendency in our minds, which can be amazingly strong, to perceive without love.

Having been taught since we were children that we are separate, finite beings, we have a very hard time when it comes to love. Love feels like a void that threatens to overwhelm us, and that's because, in a certain sense, it is and it does. It overwhelms our small self, our lonely sense of separateness. Since that sense of separateness is who we think we are, we feel like we'll die without it.

What's dying is the frightened mind, so the love inside us can get a chance to breathe.

In Course terminology, our entire network of fearful perceptions, all stemming from that first false belief in our separation from God and one another, is called the ego. The word "ego" is used differently here than the way in which it is often used in modern psychology. It is being used as the ancient Greeks used it—as the notion of a small, separated self. It is a false belief about ourselves, a lie about who and what we really are. Even though that lie is our neurosis, and living that lie is a terrible anxiety, it's amazing how resistant we are to healing the split.

Thought separated from love is a profound miscreation. It's our own power turned against ourselves. The moment the mind first deviated from love—when the Son of God forgot to laugh—an entire illusionary world came into being. *A Course in Miracles* calls this moment our "detour into fear," or "separation from God."

The ego has a pseudo-life of its own, and like all life forms, fights hard for its survival. As uncomfortable as our life might be, as painful or even desperate at times, the life we're living is the life we know, and we cling to the old rather than try something new. Most of us are so sick of ourselves, in one way or another. It's unbelievable how tenaciously we cling to what we've prayed to be released from. The ego is like a virus in the computer that attacks the core system. It seems to show us a dark parallel universe, a realm of fear and pain that doesn't actually exist but certainly seems to. Lucifer was the most beautiful angel in Heaven before he fell. The ego is our self-love turned into self-hatred.

The ego is like a gravitational force field, built up over eons of fearful thinking, which draws us away from the love in our hearts. The ego is our mental power turned against ourselves. It is clever, like we are, and smooth-talking, like we are, and manipulative, like we are. Remember all the talk about a silver-tongued devil? The ego doesn't come up to us and say, "Hi, I'm your self-loathing." It's not stupid, because we're not. Rather, it says things like, "Hi, I'm your adult, mature, rational self. I'll help you look out for number one." Then it proceeds to counsel us to look out for ourselves, at the expense of others. It teaches us selfishness, greed, judgment, and small-mindedness. But remember, there's only one of us here: What we give to others, we give to ourselves. What we withhold from others, we withhold from ourselves. In any moment when we choose fear instead of love, we deny ourselves the experience of Paradise. To the extent that we abandon love, to that extent we will feel it has abandoned us.

4.   HOLY SPIRIT

"The Holy Spirit is the call to awaken and be glad."

The power of the mind is itself neutral. It is the power given to us freely by God. We have the free will to think whatever we want to think, but no thoughts are neutral. There is no such thing as an idle thought. All thought creates form on some level. Nothing can deprive us of our own creativity. We are personally responsible for what direction we apply it in.

Taking responsibility for our lives, then, means taking responsibility for our thoughts. And praying to God to "save" our lives, means praying for Him to save us from our own negative thoughts.

Since only God exists, and everything else is an illusion, then the effects of lovelessness are only happening within the ego's hallucination. The word "sin" means loveless perception. It is an archery term. It means "you missed the mark." So God isn't angry at our sins because they're not really happening. He doesn't see sins, but only errors in perception. He doesn't want to punish us, but to heal us. The way He heals us is through a force of consciousness called the Holy Spirit.

The Course teaches that the Holy Spirit was created in the moment when the first fearful thought was thought. As perfect love, God corrects all mistakes the moment they occur. He couldn't force us back to love, because love doesn't force. It does, however, create alternatives. The Holy Spirit is God's alternative to fear.

The Holy Spirit was God's answer to the ego. He is God's "eternal communication link with His separated Sons," a bridge back to gentle thoughts, "the great Transformer of Perception." Often the Holy Spirit is referred to as the "Comforter." God can't force His way back into our thinking, because that would be violating our free will. But the Holy Spirit is a force of consciousness within us that "delivers us from Hell," or fear, whenever we consciously ask Him to, working with us on the Causal level, transforming our thoughts from fear to love. We cannot call on him in vain. Having been created by God, He's built into the computer. He comes to us in many forms, from a conversation with a friend to a serious spiritual path; from a lyric in a song to an excellent therapist. He is the inexorable drive toward wholeness that exists within, no matter how disoriented or crazy we get. Something within us always longs to go home, and He is that something.

The Holy Spirit guides us to a different perception of reality: one that is based on love. His correction of our perception is called the Atonement. He reminds us that, in every situation, the love you've given is real, and the love you have received is real. Nothing else exists. Anything other than love is an illusion. In order to escape the illusion and find inner peace, remember that only love in a situation is real. Everything else is a mistake and does not exist. It must be forgotten. We must consciously be willing to let it go.

The only thing lacking in any situation is our own awareness of love. In asking the Holy Spirit to help us, we are expressing our willingness to perceive a situation differently. We give up our own interpretations and opinions, and ask that they be replaced by His. When in pain, we pray, "Dear God, I am willing to see this differently."

Surrendering a situation to God means surrendering to Him our *thoughts* about it. What we give to God, He gives back to us renewed through the vision of the Holy Spirit. Some people think that if we surrender to God, we're giving up personal responsibility. But the opposite is true. We're taking the ultimate responsibility for a situation by being responsible for our thoughts about it. We're responsible enough to know that, when left to our own mental devices, we will instinctively respond from fear. We're responsible enough to ask for help.

Sometimes people think that calling on God means inviting a force into our lives that will make everything rosy. The truth is, it means inviting everything into our lives that will force us to grow—and growth can be messy. The purpose of life is to grow into our perfection. Once we call on God, everything that could anger us is on the way. Why? Because the place where we go into anger instead of love, is our wall. Any situation that pushes our buttons is a situation where we don't yet have the capacity to be unconditionally loving. It's the Holy Spirit's job to draw our attention to that, and help us move beyond that point.

Our comfort zones are the limited areas in which we find it *easy* to love. It's the Holy Spirit's job not to respect those comfort zones, but to bust them. We're not at the mountaintop until *any* zone is comfortable. Love isn't love until it's unconditional. We're not experiencing who we really are until we experience our perfect love.

In order to insure our progress toward the goal of enlightenment, the Holy Spirit has a highly individualized curriculum for everyone. Every encounter, every circumstance can be used by Him for His purposes. He translates between our perfect cosmic self and our worldly insanity. He enters into the illusion and leads us beyond it. He uses love to create more love, and He responds to fear as a call for love.

The Holocaust was not God's will, nor is AIDS. Both of them are products of fear. When we invite the Holy Spirit into these situations, however, He uses them as reasons and opportunities for us to grow into the very level of deep love through which they are eradicated from the earth. They challenge us to love more deeply than we have ever loved before.

If we really desire a moral answer to the Holocaust, we do everything in our power to create a world in which it could never happen again. As any thinking person knows, Hitler did not act alone. He could never have done what he did without the help of thousands of people who, although they did not share his evil vision, did not have the moral fiber to say no to it. What would the Holy Spirit have us do now? Although we cannot guarantee that a Hitler will never again be born, we can in fact create a world in which, even if a Hitler appeared, there would be so much love that hardly anyone would listen or conspire with him.

The spiritual path, then, is simply the journey of living our lives. Everyone is on a spiritual path; most people just don't know it. The Holy Spirit is a force in our minds that knows us in our perfectly loving, natural state—which we've forgotten—but enters into the world of fear and illusion with us, and uses our experiences here to remind us who we are. He does this by showing us the possibility of a loving purpose in everything we think and do. He revolutionizes our sense of why we are on the earth. He teaches us to see love as our only function. Everything we do in our lives will be used, or interpreted, by the ego or the Holy Spirit. The ego uses everything to lead us further into anxiety. The Holy Spirit uses everything to lead us into inner peace.

5. ENLIGHTENED BEINGS

"Enlightenment is but a recognition, not a change at all."

There are people who have lived on the earth, and perhaps there are people living here now, whose minds have been completely healed by the Holy Spirit. They have accepted the Atonement. In all religions, there are stories of saints or prophets who worked miracles. That is because, when the mind returns to God, it becomes a vessel for His power. The power of God transcends the laws of this world. Saints and prophets, by accepting the Atonement, have actualized the Christ within them. They have been purified of fearful thoughts and only love remains within their minds. These purified beings are called the Enlightened ones. Light means understanding. The enlightened "understand."

Enlightened people don't have anything we don't have. They have perfect love inside, and so do we. The difference is that they don't have anything *else*. Enlightened beings—Jesus and others—exist in a state that is only potential in the rest of us. The Christ-mind is merely the perspective of unconditional love. You and I have the Christ-mind in us as much as Jesus does. The difference between him and us is that we are tempted to deny it. He's beyond that. His every thought and action stems from love. The unconditional love, or Christ within him, is the truth that sets us free, because it's the perspective that saves us from our own fearful thoughts.

Jesus and other enlightened masters are our evolutionary elder brothers. According to the laws of evolution, a species develops in a certain direction until that development is no longer well adapted for survival. At that point, a mutation occurs. Although the mutation doesn't represent the majority of the species, it represents the line of evolution better adapted for the species' survival. The descendants of the mutation are then the ones to survive.

Our species is in trouble because we fight too much. We fight ourselves, each other, our planet, and God. Our fear-ridden ways are threatening our survival. A thoroughly loving person is like an evolutionary mutation, manifesting a being that puts love first and thus creates the context in which miracles occur. Ultimately, that is the only *smart* thing to do. It is the only orientation in life which will support our survival.

The mutations, the enlightened ones, show the rest of us our evolutionary potential. They point the way. There is a difference between a wayshower and a crutch. Sometimes people claim they don't need a crutch like Jesus. But he's not a crutch; he's a teacher. If you want to be a writer, you read the classics. If you want to make great music, you listen to music composed by great musicians who have gone before. If you're studying to be a painter, it's a good idea to study the great masters. If Picasso came into your room while you were learning to draw and said, "Hi, I have a couple of hours . . . would you like some hints?" would you say *no*?

So it is with spiritual masters: Jesus, Buddha, or any other enlightened being. They were geniuses in the way they used their minds and hearts, just as Beethoven was a genius with music, or Shakespeare a genius with words. Why not learn from them, follow their lead, study what they were doing right?

A Course in Miracles uses traditional Christian terminology, but it uses it in very non-traditional ways. Words like Christ, Holy Spirit, salvation, Jesus, etc., are used for their psychological rather than religious significance. As a student and teacher of *A Course in Miracles*, I have learned much about the resistance that many people have to Christian terms. As a Jew, I thought it was only other Jews who would have a problem with the word "Jesus." But I was wrong. It's not just Jews who get nervous at the mention of his name. Say the word "Jesus" to a group of moderate Christians, and there is likely to be as much resistance to the topic as there is in anyone else.

I understand why. As it says in the Course, "some bitter idols have been made of him who would be only brother to the world." So many Christian terms have been used to create and perpetuate guilt, that many thinking people have decided to reject them entirely. In many cases, in fact, the problem is worse for Christians than it is for Jews. Jewish children are usually taught nothing at all about Christian terms. For many Christian children, on the other hand, these words were charged with guilt, punishment, and fear of hell.

Words are just words, and new ones can always be found to replace ones that offend. In the case of Jesus, however, the problem isn't as simple as just coming up with another word. Jesus is his name. There's no point in pretending that his name is Herbert. By automatically rejecting Jesus, based on what some traditional Christians have done with and in his name, many people have thrown out the baby with the bath water. In relation to *A Course in Miracles* and other esoteric presentations of Christic philosophy, they have rejected the material offhand based on its language. They have fallen into a mental trap which in Alcoholics Anonymous is called "contempt prior to investigation."

Years ago, I was attending a dinner party in New York City. The topic of conversation at the table was a novel that had recently been published. Someone asked me if I had read it. I hadn't, but I had read the book review in the *New York Times*. I lied and said, "Yes." I was so appalled at myself. I hadn't read the book, but I had enough information to pretend, for a moment, that I had. I was willing to let someone else's opinion stand in for my own.

Not long after that, I thought of that incident when I was deciding whether or not to read a book—namely, *A Course in Miracles*—that dealt in any way with Jesus. I hadn't learned anything about him as a child. I had simply been told "We don't read that, dear." But Jews are also known for encouraging intellectual achievement in their children. I had been taught—although you would never have known it the night of that party—to read, and to think for myself—and so I did. To me, *A Course in Miracles* does not push Jesus. Although the books come from him, it is made very clear that you can be an advanced student of the Course and not relate personally to him at all.

The Course understands our resistances but it doesn't cater to them. It is time for a huge revolution in our understanding of Christic philosophy, and most particularly in our understanding of Jesus. The Christian religion has no monopoly on the Christ, or on Jesus himself. In every generation, we must rediscover truth for ourselves.

Who is Jesus? He is a personal symbol of the Holy Spirit. Having been totally healed by the Holy Spirit, He has become one with Him. He's not the only face the

Holy Spirit takes. He is *a* face. He is definitely a top of the mountain experience, but that's not to say he's the only one up there.

Jesus lived within this world of fear, and perceived only love. Every action, every word, every thought was guided by the Holy Spirit instead of the ego. He was a thoroughly purified being. To think about him is to think about, and so to call forth, the perfect love inside ourselves.

Jesus reached total actualization of the Christ mind, and was then given by God the power to help the rest of us reach that place within ourselves. As he says in the Course, "I am in charge of the process of Atonement." Sharing God's vision of things, he has *become* that vision. He sees each one of us as God sees us—innocent and perfect, loving and lovable—and he teaches us to see ourselves that way. That is how he leads us out of hell and into Heaven. To see with his eyes is to atone for our errors in perception. That is the miracle he works in our lives, the mystical light that bursts forth within our souls. Our minds were created as altars to God's Son. He represents God's Son. To worship Him is to worship the potential for perfect love which lies within us all.

Fairy tales are mystical allusions to the power of the inner self, handed down from generation to generation. They are stories of transformation. Tales like Snow White and Sleeping Beauty are metaphors for the relationship between the ego and the divine mind. The wicked step-mother, which is the ego, can put the Sleeping Beauty or Christ within us to sleep, but she can never destroy it. What is created by God is indestructible. The most destructive thing she can do is to cast a spell over us, to put the beauty to sleep. And so she does. But the love inside us doesn't die; it just falls asleep for a very long time. In every fairy tale, the Prince arrives. His kiss reminds us who we are, and why we came here. Prince Charming is the Holy Spirit, and He comes, in various guises and in various suits of clothes, to awaken us with His love. Just when it seems all hope is lost, when it seems as though evil has triumphed at last, our Savior appears and takes us in his arms. He has many faces, and one of them is Jesus. He is not an idol, or a crutch. He is our elder brother. He is a gift.

CHAPTER 4

Surrender

"For in God's hands we rest untroubled . . ."

1. FAITH

"There is no problem in any situation that faith will not solve."

What if we truly believed there is a God—a beneficent order to things, a force that's holding things together without our conscious control? What if we could see, in our daily lives, the working of that force? What if we believed it loved us somehow, and cared for us, and protected us? What if we believed we could afford to relax?

The physical body is at work every moment, an array of mechanisms with a brilliance of design and efficiency our human efforts have never begun to match. Our hearts beat, our lungs breathe, our ears hear, our hair grows. And we don't have to make them work—they just do. Planets revolve around the sun, seeds become flowers, embryos become babies, and with no help from us. Their movement is built into a natural system. You and I are integral parts of that system, too. We can let our lives be directed by the same force that makes flowers grow—or we can do it ourselves.

To trust in the force that moves the universe is faith. Faith isn't blind, it's visionary. Faith is believing that the universe is on our side, and that the universe knows what it's doing. Faith is a psychological awareness of an unfolding force for good, constantly at work in all dimensions. Our attempts to direct this force only interferes with it. Our willingness to relax into it allows it to work on our behalf. Without faith, we're frantically trying to control what it is not our business to control, and fix what it is not in our power to fix. What we're trying to control is much better off without us, and what we're trying to fix can't be fixed by us anyway. Without faith, we're wasting time.

There are objective, discernible laws of physical phenomena. Take gravity, for instance, or the law of thermodynamics. You don't exactly have faith in the law of gravity, so much as you just know that it is.

There are objective, discernible laws of non-physical phenomena, as well. These two sets of laws—those which rule both the external and internal worlds—are parallel.

Externally, the universe supports our physical survival. Photosynthesis in plants and plankton in the ocean produce the oxygen that we need in order to breathe. It is important to respect the laws that rule the physical universe because violation of these laws threatens our survival. When we pollute the oceans or destroy plant life, we are destroying our support system and so are destroying ourselves.

Internally, the universe supports our survival as well—emotionally and psychologically. The internal equivalent to oxygen, what we need in order to survive, is love. Human relationships exist to produce love. When we pollute our relationships with unloving thoughts, or destroy or abort them with unloving attitudes, we are threatening our emotional survival.

So the laws of the universe merely describe the way things are. These laws aren't invented; they're discovered. They are not dependent on our faith. Faith in them merely shows we understand what they are. Violation of these laws doesn't bespeak a lack of goodness; just a lack of intelligence. We respect the laws of nature in order to survive. And what is the highest internal law? That we love one another. Because if we don't, we will all die. As surely as a lack of oxygen will kill us, so will a lack of love.

2. RESISTANCE

> *"Faithlessness is not lack of faith but faith in nothing."*

A Course in Miracles tells us that there is no such thing as a faithless person. Faith is an aspect of consciousness. We either have faith in fear or we have faith in love, faith in the power of the world or faith in the power of God.

We've basically been taught that it's our job as responsible adults to be active, to be masculine in nature—to go out and get the job, to take control of our lives, to take the bull by the horns. We've been taught that that's our power. We think we're powerful because of what we've achieved rather than because of what we are. So we're caught in a Catch-22: we feel powerless to achieve until we already have.

If somebody comes along and suggests that we go with the flow, maybe lighten up a little, we really feel hysterical. After all, we're total underachievers as is, as far as we can see. The last thing we can imagine doing is becoming any more passive than we already are.

Passive energy has its own kind of strength. Personal power results from a balance of masculine and feminine forces. Passive energy without active energy becomes lazy, but active energy without passive energy becomes tyrannous. An overdose of male, aggressive energy is macho, controlling, unbalanced, and unnatural. The problem is that aggressive energy is what we've all been taught to respect. We've been taught that life was made for quarterbacks so we exalt our masculine consciousness, which, when untempered by the feminine, is hard. Therefore, so are we—all of us, men and women. We've created a fight mentality. We're always fighting for something: for the job, the money, the relationship, to get out of the relationship, to lose weight, to get sober, to get them to understand, to get them to stay, to get them to leave, and on and on. We never put away our swords.

The feminine, surrendered place in us is passive. It doesn't *do* anything. The spiritualization process— in men as well as women—is a feminization process, a quieting of the mind. It is the cultivation of personal magnetism.

If you have a pile of iron shavings and you want to arrange them in beautiful patterns, you can do one of two things. You can use your fingers and try to arrange the tiny pieces of iron into beautiful, gossamer lines—or you can buy a magnet. The magnet will attract the iron shavings. It symbolizes our feminine consciousness, which exerts its power through attraction rather than activity.

This attractive, receptive, feminine aspect of our consciousness is the space of mental surrender. In Taoist philosophy, "yin" is the feminine principle, representing the forces of the earth, while "yang" is the masculine principle, representing spirit. When God is referred to as "He," then all mankind becomes "She." This isn't a man-woman issue. Reference to God as masculine principle in no way impinges on feminist conviction. Our feminine self is just as important as our masculine.

The right relationship between male and female principle is one in which the feminine surrenders to the masculine. Surrender is not weakness or loss. It is a powerful nonresistance. Through openness and receptivity on the part of human consciousness, spirit is allowed to infuse our lives, to give them meaning and direction. In Christic philosophical terms, Mary symbolizes the feminine within us, which is impregnated by God. The female allows this process and is fulfilled by surrendering into it. This is not weakness on her part; it is strength. The Christ on earth is fathered by God, and mothered by our humanness. Through a mystical connection between the human and divine, we give birth to our higher Self.

3.   GIVING UP RESULTS

> *"You will never lose your way for God leads you."*

When we surrender to God, we surrender to something bigger than ourselves—to a universe that knows what it's doing. When we stop trying to control events, they fall into a natural order, an order that works. We're at rest while a power much greater than our own takes over, and it does a much better job than we could have done. We learn to trust that the power that holds galaxies together can handle the circumstances of our relatively little lives.

Surrender means, by definition, giving up attachment to results. When we surrender to God, we let go of our attachment to how things happen on the outside and we become more concerned with what happens on the inside.

The experience of love is a choice we make, a mental decision to see love as the only real purpose and value in any situation. Until we make that choice, we keep striving for results that we think would make us happy. But we've all gotten things that we thought would make us happy, only to find that they didn't. This external searching—looking to anything other than love to complete us and to be the source of our happiness—is the meaning of idolatry. Money, sex, power, or any other worldly satisfaction offers just temporary relief for minor existential pain.

"God" means love, and "will" means thought. God's will, then, is loving thought. If God is the source of all good, then the love within us is the source of all good. When we love, we are automatically placing ourselves within an attitudinal and behavioral context that leads to an unfoldment of events at the highest level of good for everyone involved. We don't always know what that unfoldment would look like, but we don't need to. God will do His part if we do ours. Our only job in every situation is to merely let go of our resistance to love. What happens then is up to Him. We've surrendered control. We're letting Him lead. We have faith He knows how.

There's a myth that some people are more faithful than others. A truer statement is that in some areas, some of us are more surrendered than others. We surrender to God first, of course, the things we don't really care that much about anyway. Some of us don't mind giving up our attachment to career goals, but there's no way we're going to surrender our romantic relationships, or vice versa. Everything we don't care that much about—fine—God can have it. But if it's really, really important, we think we better handle it ourselves.

The truth is, of course, that the more important it is to us, the more important it is to surrender. That which is surrendered is taken care of best. To place something in the hands of God is to give it over, mentally, to the protection and care of the beneficence of the universe. To keep it ourselves means to constantly grab and clutch and manipulate. We keep opening the oven to see if the bread is baking, which only ensures that it never gets a chance to.

Where we have an attachment to results, we tend to have a hard time giving up control. But how can we know what result to try to achieve in a situation when we don't know what's going to happen tomorrow? What do we ask for? Instead of, "Dear God, please let us fall in love, or please give me this job," we say, "Dear God, my desire, my priority is inner peace. I want the experience of love. I don't know what would bring that to me. I leave the results of this situation in your hands. I trust your will. May your will be done. Amen."

I used to feel I couldn't afford to relax because God had more important things to think about than my life. I finally realized that God is not capricious, but is rather an impersonal love for all life. My life is no more or less precious to Him than is anyone else's. To surrender to God is to accept the fact that He loves us and provides for us, because he loves and provides for all life. Surrender doesn't obstruct our power; it enhances it. God is merely the love within us, so returning to Him is a return to ourselves.

4.   THE SURRENDERED LIFE

"Holy Child of God, when will you learn that only holiness can content you and give you peace?"

To relax, to feel the love in your heart and keep to that as your focus in every situation—that's the meaning of spiritual surrender. It changes us. We become deeper, more attractive people.

In Zen Buddhism, there's a concept called "zen mind," or "beginner's mind." They say that the mind should be like an empty rice bowl. If it's already full, then the universe can't fill it. If it's empty, it has room to receive. This means that when we think we have things already figured out, we're not teachable. Genuine insight can't dawn on a mind that's not open to receive it. Surrender is a process of emptying the mind.

In the Christic tradition, this is the meaning of "becoming as a little child." Little children don't think they know what things mean. In fact, they know they don't know. They ask someone older and wiser to explain things to them. We're like children who don't know, but think we do.

The wise person doesn't pretend to know what it's impossible to know. "I don't know" can be an empowering statement. When we go into a situation not knowing, there is something inside us which *does*. With our conscious mind, we step back in order that a higher power within us can step forward and lead the way.

We need less posturing and more genuine charisma. Charisma was originally a religious term, meaning "of the spirit," or "inspired." It's about letting God's light shine through us. It's about a sparkle in people that money can't buy. It's an invisible energy with visible effects. To let go, to just love, is not to fade into the wallpaper. Quite the contrary, it's when we truly become bright. We're letting our own light shine.

We are meant to be this way. We are meant to shine. Look at small children. They're all so unique before they start *trying* to be, because they demonstrate the power of genuine humility. This is also the explanation of "beginner's luck." When we go into a situation not knowing the rules, we don't pretend to know how to figure anything out, and we don't know yet what there is to be afraid of. This releases the mind to create from its own higher power. Situations shift gear and lights go on simply because our minds have opened up to receive love. We have gotten out of our own way.

Love is a win-mode, a successful and attractive vibration. We think that success is difficult, and so, for us, it is. Success in life doesn't have to involve negative tension. We don't have to be struggling all the time. If you think about it, "taking the bull by the horns" would be a very dangerous thing to do. In fact, ambitious tension actually limits our ability to succeed because it keeps us in a state of contraction, emotionally and physically. It seems to give us energy but doesn't really, like the white sugar of mental health; there's a short high, followed by a crash. The cultivation of mental rest, or surrender, is like eating healthy food. It doesn't give us an immediate rush, but over time it provides a lot more energy.

This doesn't require sitting in a lotus position all day. We still get excited, but more gently. Many people associate a spiritual life with a grade B movie, but God doesn't get rid of all the drama in our lives. He just gets rid of the *cheap* drama. There is no higher drama than true personal growth. Nothing could be more genuinely dramatic than boys becoming real men and girls becoming real women.

Something amazing happens when we surrender and just love. We melt into another world, a realm of power already within us. The world changes when we change. The world softens when we soften. The world loves us when we choose to love the world.

Surrender means the decision to stop fighting the world, and to start loving it instead. It is a gentle liberation from pain. But liberation isn't about breaking out of anything; it's a gentle melting into who we really are. We let down our armor, and discover the strength of our Christ self. *A Course in Miracles* tells us that although we think that without the ego, all would be chaos, the opposite is true. Without the ego, all would be love.

We are simply asked to shift focus and to take on a more gentle perception. That's all God needs. Just one sincere surrendered moment, when love matters more than anything, and we know that nothing else really matters at all. What He gives us in return for our openness to Him, is an outpouring of His power from deep within us. We are given His power to share with the world, to heal all wounds, to awaken all hearts.

CHAPTER 5

Miracles

*"Your holiness reverses all the laws of the world.
It is beyond every restriction of time, space,
distance, and limits of any kind."*

1. FORGIVENESS

*"Before the glorious radiance of the kingdom,
guilt melts away, and transformed into
kindness will nevermore be what it was."*

"Miracles occur naturally as expressions of love." They reflect a shift in how we think, releasing the power of the mind to the processes of healing and correction.

This healing takes many forms. Sometimes a miracle is a change in material conditions, such as physical healing. At other times, it is a psychological or emotional change. It is a shift not so much in an objective situation—although that often occurs—as it is a shift in how we *perceive* a situation. What changes, primarily, is how we hold an experience in our minds—how we experience the experience.

The world of the human storyline, of all our concentration on behavior and all the things that occur outside us, is a world of illusion. It's a veil in front of a more real world, a collective dream. A miracle is not a rearrangement of the figures in our dream. A miracle is our awakening from it.

In asking for miracles, we are seeking a practical goal: a return to inner peace. We're not asking for something outside us to change, but for something inside us to change. We're looking for a softer orientation to life.

Old Newtonian physics claimed that things have an objective reality separate from our perception of them. Quantum physics, and particularly Heisenberg's Uncertainty Principle, reveal that, as our perception of an object changes, the object itself literally changes. The science of religion is actually the science of consciousness, because ultimately all creation is expressed through the mind. Thus, as *A Course in Miracles* says, our greatest tool for changing the world is our capacity to change our mind about the world.

Because thought is the creative level of things, changing our minds is the ultimate personal empowerment. Although it is a human decision to choose love instead of fear, the radical shift that this produces in every dimension of our lives is a gift from God. Miracles are an intercession on behalf of our holiness, from a thought system beyond our own. In the presence of love, the laws that govern the normal state of affairs are transcended. Thought that is no longer limited, brings experience that is no longer limited.

We are heir to the laws that govern the world we believe in. If we think of ourselves as beings of this world, then the laws of scarcity and death, which rule this world, will rule us. If we think of ourselves as children of God, whose real home lies in a realm of awareness beyond this world, then we will find we are "under no laws but God's."

Our self-perception determines our behavior. If we think we're small, limited, inadequate creatures, then we tend to behave that way, and the energy we radiate reflects those thoughts no matter what we do. If we think we're magnificent creatures with an infinite abundance of love and power to give, then we tend to behave that way. Once again, the energy around us reflects our state of awareness.

Miracles themselves are not to be consciously directed. They occur as involuntary effects of a loving personality, an invisible force that emanates from someone whose conscious intention is to give and receive love. As we relinquish the fears that block the love within us, we become God's instruments. We become His miracle workers.

God, as love, is constantly expanding, flourishing and creating new patterns for the expression and attainment of joy. When our minds, through focus on love, are allowed to be open vessels through which God expresses, our lives become the canvases for the expression of that joy. That's the meaning of our lives. We are here as physical representations of a divine principle. To say that we're on the earth to serve God, means that we're on the earth to love.

We weren't just randomly thrown onto a sea of

rocks. We have a mission—to save the world through the power of love. The world needs healing desperately, like a bird with a broken wing. People know this, and millions have prayed.

God heard us. He sent help. He sent you.

To become a miracle worker means to take part in a spiritual underground that's revitalizing the world, participating in a revolution of the world's values at the deepest possible level. That doesn't mean you announce this to anyone. A member of the French underground didn't walk up to a German officer occupying Paris and say, "Hi, I'm Jacques. French Resistance." Similarly, you don't tell people who would have no idea what you're talking about, "I'm changed. I'm working for God now. He sent me to heal things. The world's about to shift big time." Miracle workers learn to keep their own counsel. Something that's important to know about spiritual wisdom is that, when spoken at the wrong time, in the wrong place, or to the wrong person, the one who speaks sounds more like a fool than a wise one.

The Course tells us of God's plan for the salvation of the world, called the plan of the teachers of God. The plan calls for God's teachers to heal the world through the power of love. This teaching has very little to do with verbal communication, and everything to do with a quality of human energy. "To teach is to demonstrate." A teacher of God is anyone who chooses to be one. "They come from all over the world. They come from all religions and from no religion. They are the ones who have answered." The adage that "many are called but few are chosen" means that everyone is called, but few care to listen. God's call is universal, going out to every mind in every moment. Not everyone, however, chooses to heed the call of his own heart. As all of us are only too aware, the loud and frantic voices of the outer world easily drown out the small still loving voice within.

Our job as a teacher of God, should we choose to accept it, is to constantly seek a greater capacity for love and forgiveness within ourselves. We do this through a "selective remembering," a conscious decision to remember only loving thoughts and let go of any fearful ones. This is the meaning of forgiveness. Forgiveness is a major cornerstone of *A Course in Miracles* philosophy. Like many of the traditional terms used in the Course, it is used in a very nontraditional way.

Traditionally, we think of forgiveness as something we are to do when we see guilt in someone. In the Course, however, we're taught that it's our function to remember that there *is* no guilt in anyone, because only love is real. It is our function to see through the illusion of guilt, to the innocence that lies beyond. "To forgive is merely to remember only the loving thoughts you gave in the past, and those that were given you. All the rest must be forgotten." We are asked to extend our perception beyond the errors that our physical perceptions reveal to us—what someone did, what someone said—to the holiness within them that only our heart reveals. Actually, then, there is nothing to forgive. The traditional notion of forgiveness—what *The Song of Prayer* calls "forgiveness-to-destroy"—is then an act of judgment. It is the arrogance of someone who sees themselves as better than someone else, or perhaps equally as sinful, which is still a misperception and the arrogance of the ego.

Since all minds are connected, then the correction of anyone's perception is on some level a healing of the entire racial mind. The practice of forgiveness is our most important contribution to the healing of the world. Angry people cannot create a peaceful planet. It amuses me to think how angry I used to get when people wouldn't sign my peace petitions.

Forgiveness is a full time job, and sometimes very difficult. Few of us always succeed, yet making the effort is our most noble calling. It is the world's only real chance to begin again. A radical forgiveness is a complete letting go of the past, in any personal relationship, as well as in any collective drama.

2.   *LIVING IN THE PRESENT*

"All your past except its beauty is gone, and nothing is left but a blessing."

God exists in eternity. The only point where eternity meets time is in the present. "The present is the only time there is." A miracle is a shift in thinking from what we might have done in the past or should be doing in the future, to what we feel free to do right here, right now. A miracle is a release from internal bondage. Our capacity for brilliance is equal to our capacity to forget the past and forget the future. That's why little children are brilliant. They don't remember the past, and they don't relate to the future. Be us as little children, that the world might finally grow up.

One of the exercises in the Course Workbook reads, "The past is over. It can touch me not." Forgiving the past is an important step in allowing ourselves the experience of miracles. The only meaning of anything in our past is that it got us here, and should be honored as such. All that is real in our past is the love we gave and the love we received. Everything else is an illusion. The past is merely a thought we have. It is literally all in our minds. The Course teaches, "Give the past to Him Who can change your mind about it for you." To surrender the past to the Holy Spirit is to ask that only loving, helpful thoughts about it remain in our minds, and all the rest be let go.

What we are left with then is the present, the only time where miracles happen. We place the past and the future as well into the hands of God. The biblical statement that "time shall be no more" means that we will one day live fully in the present, without obsessing about past or future.

The universe provides us with a clean slate in every moment; God's creation holds nothing against us. Our problem is that we don't believe this. Let us ask forgiveness, not of God who has never condemned us, but of ourselves, for all we think we did and did not do. Let us give ourselves permission to begin again.

We all encounter situations in our lives where we wish we hadn't done something we did, or wish we had done something we didn't. They're those moments in our lives, be they yesterday or several years ago, that make us cringe to think about. One of the most freeing techniques provided us in *A Course in Miracles* is a prayer on page 83 of the Text, in which we instruct the universe to undo our errors:

> ". . . the first step in the undoing is to recognize that you actively decided wrongly, but can as actively decide otherwise. Be very firm with yourself in this, and keep yourself fully aware that the undoing process, which does not come from you, is nevertheless within you because God placed it there. Your part is merely to return your thinking to the point at which the error was made, and give it over to the Atonement in peace. Say this to yourself as sincerely as you can, remembering that the Holy Spirit will respond fully to your slightest invitation:

> I must have decided wrongly, because I am not at peace.

> *I made the decision myself, but I can also decide*
> *otherwise.*
> *I want to decide otherwise, because I want to be*
> *at peace.*
> *I do not feel guilty, because the Holy Spirit will*
> *undo all consequences of my wrong decision*
> *if I will let Him.*
> *I choose to let Him, by allowing Him to decide*
> *for God for me."*

And that's it! It's a course in *miracles*, not a course in moving the furniture. Miracles reverse physical laws. Time and space are under His command.

As for the future, the Course points out that there is no way for us to know what's going to happen tomorrow, or the next day, or five years from now. Only the ego speculates about tomorrow. In Heaven, we place our future in the hands of God. The Holy Spirit returns our minds to total faith and trust, that should we live with fully open hearts today, tomorrow will take care of itself. As Jesus said in the Sermon on the Mount, "Be ye not anxious for tomorrow, for tomorrow shall be anxious for itself."

"The ego bases its perception of reality on what has happened in the past, carries those perceptions into the present and thus creates a future like the past." If we felt that we were lacking in our past, our thoughts about the future are based on those perceptions. We then enter the present in an effort to compensate for the past. Since that perception is our core belief, we recreate its conditions in the future. "Past, present and future are not continuous, unless you force continuity upon them." In the present, we have the opportunity to break the continuity of the past and future by asking the Holy Spirit to intervene. This is the miracle. We want a new life, a new beginning. We desire a life untainted by any darkness of the past, and being entitled to miracles, we are entitled to that full release. This is what it means to say that Jesus washes us clean of our sins. He completely removes all loveless thoughts. We relinquish any thoughts of judgment, of anyone or anything, that hold us to the past. We relinquish any thoughts of attachment that keep us grasping at the future.

The world of the ego is a world of constant changes, ups and downs, darkness and light. Heaven is a realm of constant peace because it is an awareness of a reality that lies beyond change. "And Heaven will not change, for birth into the holy present is salvation from change."

The world that the Holy Spirit reveals to us is a world that lies beyond this world, a world revealed to us through a different perception. We die to one world in order to be born into another. "To be born again is to let the past go, and look without condemnation upon the present." The world of time is not the real world, and the world of eternity is our real home. We are on our way there. We are pregnant with possibilities.

3. RESURRECTION

"Your resurrection is your awakening."

The purpose of our lives is to give birth to the best which is within us.

The Christ comes as a little child because the symbol of the newborn infant is the symbol of someone whose innocence is unmarred by past history or guilt. The Christ child within us has no history. It is the symbol of a person who is given the chance to begin again. The only way to heal the wounds of the past, ultimately, is to forgive them and let them go. The miracle worker sees that his purpose in life is to be used in the service of the forgiveness of mankind—to awaken us from our collective sleep.

The Course tells us: "The Bible says that a deep sleep fell upon Adam, and nowhere is there reference to his waking up." So far, there has been no "comprehensive reawakening or rebirth." We can all contribute to a global rebirth to the extent that we allow ourselves to be awakened from our own personal dream of separation and guilt, to release our own past and accept a new life in the present. It is only through our own personal awakening that the world can be awakened. We cannot give what we don't have.

We're all assigned a piece of the garden, a corner of the universe that is ours to transform. Our corner of the universe is our own life—our relationships, our homes, our work, our current circumstances—exactly as they are. Every situation we find ourselves in is an opportunity, perfectly planned by the Holy Spirit, to teach love instead of fear. Whatever energy system we find ourselves a part of, it's our job to heal it—to purify the thought forms by purifying our own. It's never really a circumstance that needs to change—it's *we* who need to change. The prayer isn't for God to change our lives, but rather for Him to change us.

That's the greatest miracle, and ultimately the only one: that you awaken from the dream of separation and become a different kind of person. People are constantly concerning themselves with what they *do*: have I achieved enough, written the greatest screenplay, formed the most powerful company? But the world will not be saved by another great novel, great movie, or great business venture. It will only be saved by the appearance of great people.

A glass vase is meant to hold water. If more water is poured into the vase than its volume can contain, then the vase will shatter. So it is with our personalities. The power of God, particularly at this time, is pouring into us at rapid pace and high velocity. If our vessel, our vehicle—our human channel—is not prepared properly through devotion and deep reverence for life, then the very power that is meant to save us begins to destroy us. Our creativity, rather than making us personally powerful, then makes us hysterical. That is why creative power—God within us—is experienced as a double-edged sword: if received with grace, it blesses us; if received without grace, it drives us insane. This is one of the reasons why so many creative people have turned to a destructive use of drugs: to actually dull the experience of the reception of God's power rather than enhance it. God's power coming into us, in a culture that had no name for that power or acknowledgment of genuine spiritual experience, so frightened us that we ran to drugs or alcohol to avoid feeling what was really happening. It was only when we were stoned that we had the courage to claim our own experience.

"Miracles are everyone's right," says *A Course in Miracles*, "but purification is necessary first." Impurities— mental or chemical—pollute the system and desecrate the altar within. Our vehicle then can't handle the experience of God. The waters of spirit rush into us, but the vase begins to crack. It's not the flow of power we have to work on—God's love is already pouring in as fast as we can handle it—but the preparedness with which we receive it.

A Course in Miracles likens us to people in a very bright room who have their fingers in front of their eyes, complaining that it's dark in here. The light has come but we don't see it. We don't realize that the present is always a chance to begin again, a light-filled moment. We respond to light as if it were darkness, and so the light turns to dark. Sometimes it is only in retrospect that we can see that we were given another chance at life, a new relationship or whatever, but because we were too busy reacting to the past, we missed the opportunity at something radically new.

When we're truly honest with ourselves, our problem is not that opportunities for success haven't appeared. God is always expanding our possibilities. We are given plenty of opportunities, but we tend to undermine them. Our conflicted energies sabotage everything. To ask for another relationship, or another job, is not particularly helpful if we're going to show up in the new situation exactly as we showed up in the last one. Until we're healed of our internal demons, our fearful mental habits, we will turn every situation into the same painful drama as the one before. Everything we do is infused with the energy with which we do it. If we're frantic, life will be frantic. If we're peaceful, life will be peaceful. And so our goal in any situation becomes inner peace. Our internal state determines our experience of our lives; our experiences do not determine our internal state.

The term "crucifixion" means the energy pattern of fear. It represents the limited, negative thinking of the ego, and how it always seeks to limit, contradict or invalidate love. The term "resurrection" means the energy pattern of love, which transcends fear by replacing it. A miracle worker's function is forgiveness. In performing our function, we become channels for resurrection.

God and man are the ultimate creative team. God is like electricity. A house can be wired for it, but if there aren't any light fixtures, what good does that do? If God is seen as electricity, then we are His lamps. It doesn't matter the size of the lamp, or its shape, or design. All that matters is that it gets plugged in. It doesn't matter who we are, or what our gifts are. All that matters is that we are willing to be used in His service. Our willingness, our conviction, give us a miraculous power. The servants of God bear the imprint of their Master.

Lamps without electricity cast no light, and electricity without lamps casts no light either. Together, however, they cast out all darkness.

4. COSMIC ADULTHOOD

"Child of God, you were created to create the good, the beautiful and the holy."

As we become purer channels for God's light, we develop an appetite for the sweetness that is possible in this world. A miracle worker is not geared toward fighting the world that is, but toward creating the world that could be.

Just treating the symptom of a problem isn't really treating it. Take nuclear bombs, for example. If we all work hard, sign enough petitions and elect new officials, then we can ban the bomb. But if we don't get rid of the hatred in our hearts, what good will that do, ultimately? Our children or our children's children will manufacture a destructive force more powerful than the bomb, if they are still carrying within them enough fear and conflict.

Everything in the physical universe becomes part of the journey into fear, or the journey back to love, depending on how it's used by the mind. What we devote to love, is used for love's purposes. So we work within the worldly illusion, politically, socially, environmentally, etc., but we recognize that the real transformation of the world comes not from what we're doing, but from the consciousness with which we're doing it. We're actually just buying time while the real transformation of global energies has a chance to kick in.

The miracle worker's purpose is spiritually grand, not personally grandiose. The high cosmic drama is not *your* career, *your* money, or any of your worldly experiences. Your career is certainly important, as is your money, your talent, your energy, and your personal relationships. But they're important only to the extent that they are devoted to God to use for His purposes. When we outgrow our immature preoccupation with the small self, we transcend our selfishness and become cosmically mature.

Until we find that cosmic maturity, we're childish. We're worrying about our car payments, our career advancements, our plastic surgery, our petty hurts, while political situations careen towards disaster and the hole in the ozone looks worse every day. Childishness is when we're so preoccupied with things that ultimately don't matter, that we lose our essential connection with things that do.

There's a difference between childish and childlike. Childlike implies spirituality, as in tenderness, and a profound not-knowing that makes us open to new impressions. Childlike is when see ourselves as children in the arms of God. We learn to step back and let Him lead the way.

God isn't separate from us, because He's the love inside our minds. Every problem, inside and out, is due to separation from love on someone's part. Thirty-five thousand people a day die of hunger on earth, and there's no dearth of food. The question is not, "What kind of God would let children starve?" but rather, "What kind of people let children starve?" A miracle worker returns the world to God by making a conscious change to a more loving way of life. Waiting with cynical resignation for the world's collapse makes us part of the problem, not the answer. We must consciously recognize that, for God, "there is no order of difficulty in miracles." Love heals all wounds. No problem is too small for God's attention, or too big for Him to handle.

Every system in the world—socially, politically, economically, biologically—is beginning to crumble under the weight of our own cruelty. Without miracles, it could be argued that the gig is up, that it's already too late to save the world. Many people are convinced that the world is headed for an inevitable major collapse. Any thinking person knows that the world is in many ways moving in a downward spiral, and an object continues to move in whatever direction it's currently headed. Only the application of a stronger counterforce can change its direction. Miracles are that counterforce. When love reaches a critical mass, when enough people become miracle-minded, the world will experience a radical shift.

This is the eleventh hour. The Course tells us that it's not up to us what we learn, but only whether we learn through joy or through pain. We *will* learn to love one another, but whether we learn it painfully or peacefully is entirely up to us. If we continue in our dark ways and we manifest nuclear war, then even if there are only five people left on the planet at the end of the conflagration, those five people will have gotten the point. They would surely look at one another and say, "Let's try to get along." But we can bypass the scenario of a nuclear Armageddon if we so desire. Most of us have already suffered our own personal Armageddons. There's no need to go through the whole thing again collectively. We can get the point later, or we can get the point now. Knowing that we have a choice is a genuinely adult understanding of the world.

After Dorothy had gone through her whole dramatic journey to Oz, the good witch told her that all she had had to do was click her heels together three times and say, "I want to go home," "I want to go home," "I want to go home." There had been no need for the long traipse down the yellow brick road. Dorothy, who I'm sure was outraged, said, "Why didn't you tell me that?" The witch replied: "You wouldn't have believed me!"

In ancient Greek tragedies, there's a common device called "Deus ex machina." The plot builds up to a disastrous climax, and just when it looks as though all hope is lost, a god appears and saves the day. That's an important piece of archetypal information. At the last moment, when things look the worst, God *does* tend to appear. Not because he has a sadistic sense of humor, waiting until we're totally desperate before showing us his muscle. He takes so long because it's not until then that we bother to think about Him. All this time, we thought we were waiting for Him. Little did we know, He was waiting for us.

5.   *REBIRTH*

> *"This is what is meant by 'The meek shall inherit the earth': They will literally take it over because of their strength."*

It is time to fulfill our purpose, to live on the earth and think only the thoughts of Heaven. Thus shall Heaven and Earth become as one. They will no longer exist as two separate states.

There are times when miraculous thinking is not easy, because our mental habit patterns are permeated with fear. When that's the case—when our anger, jealousy or hurt seem stuck to our hearts and we can't let them go—how do we work miracles then? By asking the Holy Spirit to help us.

The Course tells us that we can do many things, but one thing we can never do is call on the Holy Spirit in vain. We are told that we don't ask God for too much; in fact, we ask for too little. Whenever we feel lost, or insane, or afraid, all we have to do is ask for His help.

The help might not come in the form we expected, or even thought we desired, but it will come, and we will recognize it by how we feel. In spite of everything, we will feel at peace.

We think there are different categories of life, such as money, health, relationships, and then, for some of us, another category called "spiritual life." But only the ego categorizes. There is really only one drama going on in life: our walk away from God, and our walk back. We simply reenact the one drama in different ways.

The Course says we think we have many different problems, but we only have one. Denying love is the only problem, and embracing it is the only answer. Love heals all of our relationships—to money, the body, work, sex, death, ourselves, and one another. Through the miraculous power of pure love, we let go our past history in any area and begin again.

If we treat miraculous principles like toys, they will be like toys in our lives. But if we treat them like the power of the universe, then such will they be for us. The past is over. It doesn't matter who we are, where we came from, what Mommy said, what Daddy did, what mistakes we made, what diseases we have, or how depressed we feel. The future can be reprogrammed in this moment. We don't need another seminar, another degree, another lifetime, or anyone's approval in order for this to happen. All we have to do is ask for a miracle and allow it to happen, not resist it. There can be a new beginning, a life unlike the past. Our relationships shall be made new. Our careers shall be made new. Our bodies shall be made new. Our planet shall be made new. So shall the will of God be done, on earth as it is in Heaven. Not later, but now. Not elsewhere, but here. Not through pain, but through peace. So be it. Amen.

PART II

Practice

CHAPTER 6

Relationships

"The Holy Spirit's temple is not a body, but a relationship."

1. THE HOLY ENCOUNTER

"When you meet anyone, remember it is a holy encounter. As you see him, you will see yourself. As you treat him, you will treat yourself. As you think of him, you will think of yourself. Never forget this, for in him you will find yourself or lose yourself."

Before I read *A Course in Miracles*, I studied many other spiritual and philosophical writings. It felt as though they led me up a huge flight of stairs to a giant cathedral inside my mind, but once I reached the top of the stairs, the door to the church was locked. The Course gave me the key that opened the door. The key, very simply, is other people.

Heaven, according to the Course, is neither a condition nor a place, but rather the "awareness of perfect oneness." Since the Father and the Son are one, then to love one is to love the other. The love of God is not outside us. There is a line in a song from the play *Les*

Miserables that says, "To love another person is to see the face of God." The "face of Christ" is the innocence and love behind the masks we all wear, and seeing that face, touching it and loving it in ourselves and others, is the experience of God. It is our divine humanness. It is the high we all seek.

In every relationship, in every moment, we teach either love or fear. "To teach is to demonstrate." As we demonstrate love towards others, we learn that we are lovable and we learn how to love more deeply. As we demonstrate fear or negativity, we learn self-condemnation and we learn to feel more frightened of life. We will always learn what we have chosen to teach. "Ideas leave not their source," which is why we are always a part of God, and why our ideas are always a part of us. If I choose to bless another person, I will always end up feeling more blessed. If I project guilt onto another person, I will always end up feeling more guilty.

Relationships exist to hasten our walk to God. When surrendered to the Holy Spirit, when He is in charge of our perceptions, our encounters become holy encounters with the perfect Son of God. *A Course in Miracles* says that everyone we meet will either be our crucifier or our savior, depending on what we choose to be to them. Focusing on their guilt drives the nails of self-loathing more deeply into our own skin. Focusing on their innocence sets us free. Since no thoughts are neutral, every relationship takes us deeper into Heaven or deeper into hell.

2. FORGIVENESS IN RELATIONSHIPS

"Forgiveness takes away what stands between your brother and yourself."

A Course in Miracles prides itself on being a practical Course with a practical goal: the attainment of inner peace. Forgiveness is the key to inner peace because it is the mental technique by which our thoughts are transformed from fear to love. Our perceptions of other people often become a battleground between the ego's desire to judge and the Holy Spirit's desire to accept people as they are. The ego is the great fault-finder. It seeks out the faults in ourselves and others. The Holy Spirit seeks out our innocence. He sees all of us as we really are, and since we are the perfect creations of God, He loves what He sees. The places in our personality where we tend to deviate from love are not our faults, but our wounds. God doesn't want to punish us, but to heal us. And that is how He wishes us to view the wounds in other people.

Forgiveness is "selective remembering"—a conscious decision to focus on love and let the rest go. But the ego is relentless—it is "capable of suspiciousness at best and viciousness at worst." It presents the most subtle and insidious arguments for casting other people out of our hearts. The cornerstone of the ego's teaching is: "The Son of God is guilty." The cornerstone of the Holy Spirit's teaching is: "The Son of God is innocent."

The miracle worker consciously invites the Holy Spirit to enter into every relationship and deliver us from the temptation to judge and find fault. We ask Him to save us from our tendency to condemn. We ask Him to reveal to us the innocence within others, that we might see it within ourselves.

"Dear God, I surrender this relationship to you," means, "Dear God, let me see this person through your eyes." In accepting the Atonement, we are asking to see as God sees, think as God thinks, love as God loves. We are asking for help in seeing someone's innocence.

I was once vacationing in Europe with my family. Although my mother and I were both making noble efforts at getting along well with each other, we weren't succeeding. Old patterns of attack and defense were continuously cropping up between us. She wanted a more conservative daughter, and I wanted a more enlightened mother. I kept opening the Course for help and inspiration but much to my chagrin, I seemed to open the book to the same section each time I picked it up. I would read, "Think honestly what you have thought that God would not have thought, and what you have not thought that God would have you think." In other words, where were my thoughts not aligned with God's? It was driving me crazy. I wanted support for my defensive feelings. The last thing I wanted to be told was that the only error was an error in my own thinking.

Finally, glancing across St. Mark's Square in Venice, I looked closely at my mother and said to myself, "It's true—God's not looking at her and thinking, 'Sophie Ann is such a bitch.' " As long as I chose to see her that way, as long as I was not willing to give up my focus on her errors, I could not be at peace because I was not sharing God's perception. As soon as I saw this, I released my tense fixation on what I perceived to be her guilt. From that point forward, the situation began to shift. Miraculously, she was nicer to me, and I was nicer to her.

It's easy to forgive people who have never done anything to make us angry. People who do make us angry, however, are our most important teachers. They indicate the limits to our capacity for forgiveness. "Holding grievances is an attack on God's plan for salvation." The decision to let go our grievances against other people is the decision to see ourselves as we truly are, because any darkness we let blind us to another's perfection also blinds us to our own.

It can be very hard to let go of your perception of someone's guilt when you know that by every standard of ethics, morality, or integrity, you're right to find fault with them. But the Course asks, "Do you prefer that you be right or happy?" If you're judging a brother, you're wrong even if you're right. There have been times when I have had a very hard time giving up my judgment of someone, mentally protesting, "But I'm *right*." I felt as though giving up my judgment amounted to condoning their behavior. I felt, "Well, *somebody's* got to uphold principle in this world. If we just forgive things all the time, then all standards of excellence will disintegrate!"

But God doesn't need us to police the universe. Shaking our finger at someone doesn't help them change. If anything, our perception of someone's guilt only keeps them stuck in it. When we are shaking a finger at someone, figuratively or literally, we are not more apt to correct their wrongful behavior. Treating someone with compassion and forgiveness is much more likely to elicit a healed response. People are less likely to be defensive, and more likely to be open to correction. Most of us are aware on some level when we're off. We'd be doing things differently if we knew how. We don't need attack at this point; we need help. Forgiveness forges a new context, one in which someone can more easily change.

Forgiveness is the choice to see people as they are *now*. When we are angry at people, we are angry because of something they said or did before this moment. But what people said or did is not who they are. Relationships are reborn as we let go perceptions of our brother's past. By bringing the past into the present, we create a future just like the past. By letting the past go, we make room for miracles.

An attack on a brother is a reminder of his guilty past. In choosing to affirm a brother's guilt, we are choosing to experience more of it. The future is programmed in the present. To let the past go is to remember that in the present, my brother is innocent. It is an act of gracious generosity to accept a person based on what we know to be the truth about them, regardless of whether or not they are in touch with that truth themselves.

Only love is real. Nothing else actually exists. If a person behaves unlovingly, then, that means that, regardless of their negativity—anger or whatever—their behavior was derived from fear and doesn't actually exist. They're hallucinating. You forgive them, then, because there's nothing to forgive. Forgiveness is a discernment between what is real and what is not real.

When people behave unlovingly, they have forgotten who they are. They have fallen asleep to the Christ within them. The job of the miracle worker is to remain awake. We choose not to fall asleep and dream of our brother's guilt. In this way we are given the power to awaken him.

A prime example of a miracle worker is Pollyanna. The ego knows this, which is why she is constantly invalidated in this culture. She walked into a situation where everyone had been in a nasty mood for years. She chose not to see the nastiness. She had faith in what lay beyond it. She extended her perception beyond what her physical senses revealed to her, to what her heart knew to be true about every human being. It didn't matter how anyone behaved. Pollyanna had faith in the love she knew existed behind anyone's fear, and thus she invoked their love into expression. She exercised the power of forgiveness. Within a short time, everyone was nice and everyone was happy! Whenever someone says to me,

"Marianne, you're being a Pollyanna," I think to myself, "If only I were that powerful."

3.   GIVING UP JUDGMENT

"Judgment is not an attribute of God."

A Course in Miracles tells us that whenever we are contemplating attacking someone, it is as though we are holding a sword above their head. The sword, however, doesn't fall on them but on us. Since all thought is thought about ourselves, then to condemn another is to condemn ourselves.

How do we escape judgment? Largely through a reinterpretation of what we're judging. *A Course in Miracles* describes the difference between a sin and an error. A sin would mean we did something so bad that God is angry at us. But since we can't do anything that changes our essential nature, God has nothing to be angry at. Only love is real. Nothing else exists. The Son of God cannot sin. We can make mistakes, to be sure, and we obviously do. But God's attitude toward error is a desire to heal us. Because we ourselves are angry and punishing, we have concocted the idea of an angry, punishing God. We are created in God's image, however, and not the other way around. As extensions of God, we are ourselves the spirit of compassion, and in our right minds, we don't seek to judge but to heal. We do this through forgiveness. When someone has behaved unlovingly—when they yell at us, or lie about us, or steal from us—they have lost touch with their essence. They have forgotten who they are. But everything that someone does, says the Course, is either love or a call for love. If someone treats us with love, then of course love is the appropriate response. If they treat us with fear, we are to see their behavior as a call for love.

The American prison system illustrates the philosophical and practical difference between the choice to perceive sin or to perceive error. We see criminals as guilty and seek to punish them. But whatever we do to others, we are doing to ourselves. Statistics painfully prove that our prisons are schools for crime; a vast number of crimes are committed by people who have already spent time in prison. In punishing others, we end up punishing ourselves. Does that mean we're to forgive a rapist, tell him we know he just had a bad day and send him home? Of course not. We're to ask for a miracle. A miracle here would be a shift from perceiving prisons as houses of punishment to perceiving them as houses of rehabilitation. When we consciously change their purpose from fear to love, we release infinite possibilities of healing.

Forgiveness is like the martial arts of consciousness. In Aikido and other martial arts, we sidestep our attacker's force rather than resisting it. The energy of the attack then boomerangs back in the direction of the attacker. Our power lies in remaining nonreactive. Forgiveness works in the same way. When we attack back, and defense is a form of attack, we initiate a war that no one can win. Since lovelessness is not real, we're not at the effect of it in ourselves or others. The problem, of course, is that we think we are. In seeking a miracle, we don't take part in life's battles, but rather we are asking to be lifted above them. The Holy Spirit reminds us that the battle is not real.

"Vengeance is mine, sayeth the Lord," means, "Relinquish the idea of vengeance." God balances all wrong, but not through attack, judgment or punishment. Contrary to how it feels when we're lost in the emotions that tempt us to judge, there's no such thing as righteous anger. When I was a little girl, I would fight with my brother or sister, and when my mother came home she would be annoyed at us for arguing. One of us would always say, "They did it first." It actually doesn't matter who "did it first." Whether you're attacking first or attacking back, you're an instrument of attack and not of love.

Several years ago I was at a cocktail party where I got into a very heated debate about American foreign policy. Later that night, I had a kind of waking dream. A gentleman appeared to me and said, "Excuse me, Miss Williamson, but we thought we should tell you: In the cosmic roll call, you are considered a hawk, not a dove."

I was incensed. "No way," I said indignantly. "I'm totally for peace. I'm a dove all the way."

"I'm afraid not," he said. "I'm looking on our charts, and it says very clearly right here: Marianne Williamson, warmonger. You're at war with Ronald Reagan, Caspar Weinberger, the CIA, in fact the entire American defense establishment. No, I'm sorry. You're definitely a hawk."

I saw, of course, that he was right. I had just as many missiles in my head as Ronald Reagan had in his. I thought it was wrong for him to judge communists, but I thought it was okay for me to judge him. Why? Because I was *right*, of course!

I spent years as an angry left-winger before I realized that an angry generation can't bring peace. Everything we do is infused with the energy with which we do it. As Gandhi said, "We must *be* the change." What the ego doesn't want us to see is that the guns we need to get rid of first are the guns in our own heads.

4. *THE CHOICE TO LOVE*

> *"The ego is the choice for guilt; the Holy Spirit the choice for guiltlessness."*

The ego always emphasizes what someone has done wrong. The Holy Spirit always emphasizes what they've done right. The Course likens the ego to a scavenger dog that seeks out every scrap of evidence for our brother's guilt and lays it at its master's feet. The Holy Spirit, similarly, sends out its own messengers to seek evidence of our brother's innocence. The important thing is that we decide what we want to see before we see it. We receive what we request. "Projection makes perception."

We can find—and in fact, we *will* find—whatever it is we're looking for in life. The Course says that we think we will understand a person enough to know whether or not they are lovable, but that unless we love them, we can never understand them. The spiritual path involves taking conscious responsibility for what we choose to perceive—our brother's guilt or innocence. We see a brother's innocence when it's all we *want* to see. People are not perfect—that is, they do not yet express externally their internal perfection. Whether we choose to focus on the guilt in their personality, or the innocence in their soul, is up to us.

What we think of as people's guilt is their fear. All negativity derives from fear. When someone is angry, they are afraid. When someone is rude, they are afraid. When someone is manipulative, they are afraid. When someone is cruel, they are afraid. There is no fear that love does not dissolve. There is no negativity that forgiveness does not transform.

Darkness is merely the absence of light, and fear is merely the absence of love. We can't get rid of darkness by hitting it with a baseball bat, because there is nothing to hit. If we want to be rid of darkness, we must turn on a light. Similarly, if we want to be rid of fear, we cannot fight it but must replace it with love.

The choice to love is not always easy. The ego puts up terrible resistance to giving up fear-laden responses. This is where the Holy Spirit comes in. It's not our job to change our own perceptions, but to remember to ask Him to change them for us.

Let's say your husband has left you for another woman. You can't change other people, and you can't ask God to change them, either. You can, however, ask to see this situation differently. You can ask for peace. You can ask the Holy Spirit to change your perceptions. The miracle is that, as you release judgment of your husband and the other woman, the pain in your gut begins to subside.

The ego might say in that situation that you'll never be at peace until your husband comes back. But peace isn't determined by circumstances outside us. Peace stems from forgiveness. Pain doesn't stem from the love we're denied by others, but rather from the love that we deny them. In a case like that, it feels as though we're hurt by what someone else did. But what really has occurred is that someone else's closed heart has tempted us to close our own, and it is our own denial of love that hurts us. That's why the miracle is a shift in our own thinking: the willingness to keep our own heart open, regardless of what's going on outside us.

A miracle is always available in any situation, because no one can decide for us how to interpret our own experience. There are only two emotions: love and fear. We can interpret fear as a call for love. Miracle workers, says the Course, are generous out of self-interest. We give someone a break so we can stay in peace ourselves.

The ego says that we can project our anger onto another person and not feel it ourselves, but since all minds are continuous, whatever we project onto another we continue to feel. Getting angry at someone else might make us feel better for a while, but ultimately all the fear and guilt comes back at us. If we judge another person, then they'll judge us back—and even if they don't, *we'll feel like they did!*

Living in this world has taught us to instinctively respond from an unnatural space, always jumping to anger, or paranoia, or defensiveness, or some other form of fear. Unnatural thinking feels natural to us, and natural thinking feels unnatural.

A Course in Miracles is not about pouring pink paint over our anger and pretending it doesn't exist. What is psychologically unsound is spiritually unsound. Denial or suppression of emotions is unsound. You don't say, "I'm not angry, really I'm not. I'm on page 140 of *A Course in Miracles* and I don't get angry anymore," when inside you're seething. The Holy Spirit tells us, "Don't try to purify yourself before coming to me. I am the purifier." I was once on my way to giving a lecture on the Course, and I thought about a woman I knew who I was feeling annoyed at. Very quickly, I tried to hide the thought, as though it wasn't holy enough for me to be thinking at such a time. Then it seemed as though a voice in my head said, "Hey, I'm your friend. Remember?" The Holy Spirit wasn't judging me for my anger; He was there to help me move past it.

We mustn't forget what the Holy Spirit is for. We don't deny we're upset, but at the same time we own up to the fact that all our feelings stem from our own loveless thinking, and we're willing to have that lovelessness healed. Growth is never about focusing on someone else's lessons, but only on our own. We aren't victims of the world outside us. As hard as it is to believe sometimes, we're always responsible for how we see things. There would be no savior if there were no need for one. Of course things happen in this world that make it almost impossible to love—cruel, horrible things—but the Holy Spirit is within us to do the impossible. He does for us what we can't do for ourselves. He will lend us His strength, and when His mind is joined with ours, ego thinking is cast out.

But we must be aware of our ego feelings in order to release them. "He cannot shine away what you keep hidden, for you have not offered it to Him and he cannot take it from you." It would be violating our free will for the Holy Spirit to change our mental patterns unasked. But when we ask Him to change them, He will. When we're angry, or upset for any reason, we're asked to say, "I'm angry but I'm willing not to be. I'm willing to see this situation differently." We ask the Holy Spirit to enter into the situation and show it to us from a different perspective.

Once I was having porcelain fingernails applied, and my manicurist's friend came into the room. I couldn't tolerate her personality. From the moment this woman opened her mouth, I felt like someone was running fingernails over a blackboard. Since my hands weren't free, I couldn't leave the room, and since the manicurist was someone who came to my lectures, I felt ashamed of my own reaction. I prayed and asked God for help. His response was dramatic. Within moments, the "obnoxious" woman began talking about her childhood, and particularly her relationship with her father. As she began to describe her upbringing, it became perfectly clear to me how she would have grown up with little self-esteem, and an inordinate need to develop grandiose personality characteristics, which in her mind would denote strength. Her defenses didn't work, of course. Coming from fear, they merely put people off. Suddenly, the same behavior that had so irritated me five minutes before, now elicited in me a deep compassion. The Holy Spirit had pointed me to the information that would melt my heart. Now I saw her differently. That was the miracle: Her behavior hadn't changed, but *I* had.

5. LEVELS OF TEACHING

"Therefore, the plan includes very specific contacts to be made for every teacher of God."

Relationships are assignments. They are part of a vast plan for our enlightenment, the Holy Spirit's blueprint by which each individual soul is led to greater awareness and expanded love. Relationships are the Holy Spirit's laboratories in which He brings together people who have the maximal opportunity for mutual growth. He appraises who can learn most from whom at any given time, and then assigns them to each other. Like a giant universal computer, He knows exactly what combination of energies, in exactly what context, would do the most to further God's plan for salvation. No meetings are accidental. "Those who are to meet will meet, because together they have the potential for a holy relationship."

The Course says that there are three levels of teaching in relationship. The first level is what we think of as a casual encounter, such as two strangers meeting in an elevator or students who "happen" to walk home from school together. The second level is a "more sustained relationship, in which, for a time, two people enter into a fairly intense teaching-learning situation and then appear to separate." The third level of teaching is a relationship which, once formed, lasts all our lives. At this level, "each person is given a chosen learning partner who presents him with unlimited opportunities for learning."

Even at the first level of teaching, the people in the elevator might smile at one another or the students might become friends. It is mostly in casual encounters that we are given a chance to practice the fine art of chiseling away the hard edges of our personalities. Whatever personal weaknesses are evident in our casual interactions will inevitably appear magnified in more intense relationships. If we're crabby with the bank teller, it will be harder to be gentle with the people we love the most.

At the second level of teaching, people are brought together for more intense work. During their time together, they will go through whatever experiences provide them with their next lessons to be learned. When physical proximity no longer supports the highest level of teaching and learning between them, the assignment will call for physical separation. What then appears to be the end of the relationship however, is not really an end. Relationships are eternal. They are of the mind, not the body, since people are energy, not physical substance. Bodies joining may or may not denote real joining, since joining is of the mind. People who have slept in the same bed for twenty-five years may not be truly joined, and people who are many miles apart may not be separate at all.

Often we see a couple who has separated or divorced and look with sadness at the "failure" of their relationship. But if both people learned what they were meant to learn, then that relationship was a success. Now it may be time for physical separation so that more can be learned in other ways. That not only means learning elsewhere, from other people; it also means learning the lessons of pure love that come from having to release the form of an existing relationship.

Third-level, life-long relationships are generally few because "their existence implies that those involved have reached a stage simultaneously in which the teaching-learning balance is actually perfect." That doesn't mean, however, that we necessarily recognize our third-level assignments; in fact, generally we don't. We may even feel hostility toward these particular people. Someone with whom we have a lifetime's worth of lessons to learn is someone whose presence in our lives forces us to grow. Sometimes it represents someone with whom we participate lovingly all our lives, and sometimes it represents someone who we experience as a thorn in our side for years, or even forever. Just because someone has a lot to teach us, doesn't mean we like them. People who have the most to teach us are often the ones who reflect back to us the limits to our own capacity to love, those who consciously or unconsciously challenge our fearful positions. They show us our walls. Our walls are our wounds—the places where we feel we can't love any more, can't connect any more deeply, can't forgive past a certain point. We are in each other's lives in order to help us see where we most need healing, and in order to help us heal.

6.   THE SPECIAL RELATIONSHIP

"The special love relationship is the ego's chief weapon for keeping you from Heaven."

We can all relate to the desire to find Mr. or Ms. Right. It's almost a cultural obsession. But according to *A Course in Miracles*, the search for the perfect person to "fix" us is one of our biggest psychic wounds, and one of the ego's most powerful delusions. It represents a notion that *A Course in Miracles* calls the "special relationship." Although the word "special" normally implies something wonderful, from a Course perspective, special means different, therefore separate, which is characteristic of ego rather than spirit. A special relationship is a relationship based on fear.

God created only one begotten Son and He loves all of us as one. To Him, no one is different or special because no one is actually separate from anyone else. Since our peace lies in loving as God loves, we must strive to love everyone. Our desire to find one "special person," one part of the Sonship who will complete us, is hurtful because it is delusional. It means we're seeking salvation in separation rather than in oneness. The only love that completes us is the love of God, and the love of God is the love of everyone. That doesn't mean that the form of our relationships is the same with everyone, but it means that we are seeking the same content in every relationship: a quality of brotherly love and friendship that goes beyond the changes of form and bodies.

Just as the Holy Spirit was God's answer to the separation, the special relationship was then the ego's answer to the creation of the Holy Spirit. After the separation, we began to feel a huge gaping hole within us, and most of us still feel it. The only antidote for this is the Atonement, or return to God, because the pain we feel is actually our own denial of love. The ego, however, tells us differently. It argues that the love we need must come from someone else, and that there's one special person out there who can fill up that hole. Since the desire for that person actually stems from our belief that we're separate from God, then the desire itself symbolizes the separation and the guilt we feel because of it. Our search then carries the energy of the separation. It becomes about guilt. This is why so much anger is often aroused in our closest relationships. We're projecting onto someone else the rage we feel against ourselves for cutting off our own love.

Often when we think we are "in love" with a person, as *A Course in Miracles* indicates, we're actually anything but. The special relationship is based not on love but on guilt. The special relationship is the ego's seductive pull away from God. It is a major form of idolatry, or temptation to think that something other than God can complete us and give us peace. The ego tells us that there is some special person out there who will make all the pain go away. We don't really believe that, of course, but then on the other hand we really do. Our culture has bred the idea into us, through books, songs, movies, advertising, and more importantly, the conspiracy of other egos. It is the job of the Holy Spirit to transform the energy of special love from treachery to holiness.

The special relationship makes other people—their behavior, their choices, their opinions of us—too important. It makes us think we need another person, when in fact we are complete and whole as we are. Special love is a "blind" love, seeking to heal the wrong wound. It addresses the gap between ourselves and God, which doesn't actually exist but which we think does. By addressing this gap as real, and displacing its source onto other people, we actually manufacture the experience we seek to rectify.

Under the Holy Spirit's guidance, we come together to share joy. Under the ego's direction, we come together to share desperation. Negativity, however, cannot really be shared because it is an illusion. "A special relationship is a kind of union from which union is excluded."

A relationship is not meant to be the joining at the hip of two emotional invalids. The purpose of a relationship is not for two incomplete people to become one, but rather for two complete people to join together for the greater glory of God.

The special relationship is a device by which the ego separates rather than joins us. Based on a belief in internal emptiness, it is always asking, "What can I get?", whereas the Holy Spirit asks, "What can I give?" The ego seeks to use other people to fulfill our needs as we define them. Certain voices go on endlessly these days about whether or not "our needs are being met" in a relationship. But when we try to use a relationship to serve our own purposes, we falter because we are reinforcing our illusion of need. Under the ego's guidance we're always looking for something, yet always sabotaging what we've found.

One of my girlfriends called me one day and said she had had a date with someone she really liked. The next week, she called and said he had broken a date with her in order to go out of town. She didn't like him after all. "I won't take that from anyone," she told me. "I'm ready for a *relationship*."

"No you're not ready for a relationship," I told her. "Not if another person isn't allowed to make a mistake, you're not."

The ego had told her to reject the man because she was ready for a relationship, but what it was really doing was to make sure she wouldn't have one. The ego isn't looking for someone to love; it's looking for someone to attack. Its dictate in love is "Seek, and do not find." It looks for a reflection of itself, another mask that hides the face of Christ. In the special relationship, I'm afraid to show you the real truth about myself—my fears, my weaknesses—because I'm afraid that if you see them, you'll leave. I'm assuming you're as judgmental as I am. And I'm also not really jumping up and down wanting to see your weak spots either because it makes me nervous to think I'm involved with someone who has them. The whole setup mitigates against authenticity and therefore against real growth. A special relationship perpetuates the self-punishing masquerade in which we all seek desperately to attract love through being someone we're not. Although we're seeking love, we're actually fostering our own self-hatred and lack of self-esteem.

What's our miracle here? It's a shift from thoughts of specialness to thoughts of holiness. Our mental patterns in regard to relationships are so fraught with fear—attack and defensiveness, guilt and selfishness, however prettily disguised—that many times we are brought to our knees. As always, that's a good place to be. We pray for God to guide our thoughts and feelings. You can place any relationship under the Holy Spirit's care and be sure that it will not result in pain.

7.   THE HOLY RELATIONSHIP

"The holy relationship is the old unholy
relationship transformed and seen anew."

If the special relationship is the ego's response to the creation of the Holy Spirit, the holy relationship is the Holy Spirit's response back. The holy relationship is the old, special relationship transformed. In the special relationship, the ego guides our thinking and we meet in fear, mask to mask. In the holy relationship, the Holy Spirit has changed our minds about the purpose of love and we meet heart to heart.

A Course in Miracles describes the difference between an unholy and a holy alliance:

> *"For an unholy relationship is based on*
> *differences, where each one thinks the other has*
> *what he has not. They come together, each to*
> *complete himself and rob the other. They stay*
> *until they think that there is nothing left to steal,*
> *and then move on. And so they wander through*
> *a world of strangers, unlike themselves, living*

with their bodies perhaps under a common roof
that shelters neither; in the same room and yet a
world apart.

A holy relationship starts from a different
premise. Each one has looked within and seen no
lack. Accepting his completion, he would extend
it by joining with another, whole as himself."

The purpose of a special relationship is to teach us to
hate ourselves, while the purpose of a holy relationship is
to heal us of our self-loathing. In the special relationship,
we are always trying to hide our weaknesses. In the holy
relationship, it's understood that we all have unhealed
places, and that healing is the purpose of our being with
another person. We don't try to hide our weaknesses,
but rather we understand that the relationship is a context for healing through mutual forgiveness. Adam and
Eve were naked in the garden of Eden but not embarrassed. That doesn't mean they were physically naked.
It means they were emotionally naked, totally real and
honest, yet they were not embarrassed because they felt
accepted completely for who they were.

The Course presents an image of the special relationship as a picture set in a frame. The ego is more interested
in the frame—the idea of the perfect person who will
"fix" everything—than we are in the picture, which is
the person himself. The frame is baroque, and decorated
with rubies and diamonds. But the Course says the rubies are our blood and the diamonds are our tears. That

is the essence of specialness. It is not love but exploitation. What we call love is often hate or at best, robbery. Although we may not know it consciously, our search is often for someone who has what we think we don't have, and once we get it from them we'll be ready to move on. In a holy relationship, we're interested in the picture itself. All we want by way of a frame is a light support that does just enough to keep the picture in place. We're not interested in our brother for what he can do for us. We're interested in our brother, period.

The holy relationship is, above all else, a friendship between two brothers. We are not put here to audition one another, put someone on trial, or use other people to gratify our own ego needs. We are not here to fix, change or belittle another person. We are here to support, forgive and heal one another. I was once counseling a couple who were in the process of messily completing their relationship. The man had moved on to date someone else and the woman was angry. During our session she said to him about the new girlfriend, "You only like her because she tells you how *wonderful* you are all the time!" He looked at her very seriously and quietly said, "Yeah, I think that has something to do with it."

How do we find a holy relationship? Not by asking God to change our partners, but by asking God to change our minds. We don't run away from someone we're attracted to because we're afraid of specialness. Anytime there's a potential for love, there's a potential for specialness. I often ask audiences, "What's the first thing we should do when we're attracted to someone?" and they reply in pep-rally fashion, "*pray!*" The prayer goes something like this: "Dear God, you know, and I know, that I have more potential for neurosis in this area than in any other. Please take my attraction, my thoughts and feelings about this person and use them for your purposes. Let this relationship unfold according to your will, Amen."

Spiritual progress is like a detoxification. Things have to come up in order to be released. Once we have asked to be healed, then our unhealed places are forced to the surface. A relationship that is used by the Holy Spirit becomes a place where our blocks to love are not suppressed or denied, but rather brought into our conscious awareness. We never get crazy like we do around the people we're really attracted to. Then we can see our dysfunctions clearly, and when we're ready, ask God to show us another way.

As temples of healing, relationships are like a trip to the divine physician's office. How can a doctor help us unless we show him our wounds? Our fearful places have to be revealed before they can be healed. *A Course in Miracles* teaches that darkness is to be brought to light, and not the other way around. If a relationship allows us to merely avoid our unhealed places, then we're hiding there, not growing. The universe will not support that.

The ego thinks of a perfect relationship as one in which everybody shows a perfect face. But this is not necessarily so, because a show of strength is not always honest. It is not always a genuine expression of who we are. If I pretend to have it together in some area where I really don't, I am fostering an illusion about myself. I would only be doing this out of fear—fear that if you saw the truth about me, I would be rejected.

God's idea of a "good relationship" and the ego's idea of one are completely different. To the ego, a good relationship is one in which another person basically behaves the way we want them to and never presses our buttons, never violates our comfort zones. But if a relationship exists to support our growth, then in many ways it exists to do just those things; force us out of our limited tolerance and inability to love unconditionally. We're not aligned with the Holy Spirit until people can behave in any way they choose to, and our own inner peace isn't shaken. There have been times in my life where my thought about a relationship was, "This is terrible," but upon further reflection I realized God would probably be saying, "Oh, this is good." Marianne gets to see, in other words, her own neuroses more clearly.

A girlfriend once told me she had broken up with her boyfriend.

"Why?" I asked.

"Because he didn't call me for five days."

I didn't say anything.

"He knows I need verbal reassurance on a daily basis," she continued. "So I set my limits. Don't you think that's good?"

"No," I said. "I think it's childish." I paused. "Have you considered accepting him as he is?"

"Well, thanks for the support," she said.

I responded, "You're welcome."

I knew she thought of support as agreement from others that her boyfriend was guilty. Support for the belief in guilt is extremely easy to find. But real support is when we help one another see beyond someone's errors, to drop our judgments and see the love that lies beyond.

Our neuroses in relationships usually stem from our having an agenda for another person, or for the relationship itself. It's not our job to try to make a relationship into something we think it should be. If someone doesn't behave like a great romantic partner, then perhaps they're not meant to be that for us. That doesn't make them wrong. Not every relationship is meant to be the ultimate romance: if the train doesn't stop at your station, it's not your train. The ego seeks to use a relationship to fill our needs as we define them; the Holy Spirit asks that the relationship be used by God to serve His purposes. And His purpose is always that we might learn how to love others more purely. We love purely when we release other people to be who they are. The ego seeks intimacy through control and guilt. The Holy Spirit seeks intimacy through acceptance and release.

In the holy relationship, we don't seek to change someone, but rather to see how beautiful they already are. Our prayer becomes "Dear God, take the scales from in front of my eyes. Help me to see my brother's beauty." It is our failure to accept people exactly as they are that gives us pain in a relationship.

Our ego is merely our fear. We all have egos, that doesn't make us bad people. Our egos are not where we are bad but where we are wounded. The Course says that we are all afraid on some level that if people saw who we really are, they would recoil in horror. That is why we invent the mask, to hide our true selves. But the true self—the Christ within us—is that which is most beautiful. We must reveal ourselves at the deepest level in order to find out how lovable we really are. When we dig deeply enough into our real nature, we do not find darkness. We find endless light. That is what the ego doesn't want us to see; that our safety actually lies in letting *down* our mask. But we cannot do this when we're constantly afraid of being judged. The holy relationship is a context where we feel safe enough to be ourselves, knowing that our darkness will not be judged but forgiven. In this way we are healed, and freed to move on into the light of our true being. We are motivated to grow. A holy relationship is this: "a common state of mind, where both give errors gladly to correction, that both may happily be healed as one."

8. ROMANTIC LOVE

"There is no love but God's."

There are no different categories of love. There isn't one kind of love between a mother and a child, another between lovers, and another between friends. The love that is real is the love that lies at the heart of all relationships. That is the love of God and it doesn't change with form or circumstance.

A girlfriend of mine remarked to me recently, "Your relationship with your baby must be showing you a whole new kind of love." "No, it's not," I replied. "But it's showing me a new depth of tenderness, which is teaching me more about what love is."

People ask, "Why can't I find a deep, intimate romance?" The question is understandable, because people are lonely. An intimate romantic love, however, is like taking graduate work toward a Ph.D. in the ways of love, and many of us are hardly out of elementary school. When we're not in a relationship, the ego makes it seem as though all the pain would go away if we were. If the relationship lasts, however, it will actually bring much of our existential pain to the surface. That's part of its purpose. It will demand all of our skills at compassion, acceptance, release, forgiveness, and selflessness. We might tend to forget the challenges involved in a relationship when we're not in one, but we remember them clearly enough once we are.

Relationships don't necessarily take the pain away. The only thing that "takes the pain away" is a healing of the things that cause the pain. It isn't the absence of other people in our lives that causes us the pain, but rather what we do with them when they're there. Pure love asks for nothing but peace for a brother, knowing that only in that way can we be at peace ourselves. How many times have I had to ask myself, "Do I want him to be at peace, or do I want him to call?" Pure love of another person is the restoration of our heartline. The ego, therefore, is marshaled against it. It will do everything it can to block the experience of love in any form. When two people come together in God, the walls that appear to separate us disappear. The beloved doesn't seem to be a mere mortal. They seem for a while to be something else, something more. The truth is, they *are* something more. No one is anything less than the perfect Son of God, and when we fall in love, we have an instant when we see the total truth about someone. They *are* perfect. That's not just our imagination.

But the craziness sets in quickly. As soon as the light appears, the ego begins its powerful drive to shut it out. All of a sudden, the perfection we glanced on the spiritual planes becomes projected onto the physical. Instead of realizing that spiritual perfection and physical, material imperfection exist simultaneously, we start looking for material, physical perfection. We think someone's spiritual perfection isn't enough. They have to have perfect clothes as well. They have to be hip. They have to dazzle. And so no one gets to be a human being anymore. We idealize one another, and when someone doesn't live up to the ideal, we're disappointed.

Rejecting another human being simply because they are human, has become a collective neurosis. People ask, "When will my soul mate get here?" But praying for the right person is useless if we're not ready to receive him.

Our soul mates are human beings, just like we are, going through the normal processes of growth. No one is ever "finished." The top of one mountain is always the bottom of another, and even if someone meets us when we feel "on top" of things, the chances are good that very soon we'll be going through something that challenges us. It is our commitment to growth that makes this inevitable. But the ego doesn't like the look of people when they're "going through things." It's unattractive. As in every other area, the problem in relationships is rarely that we haven't had wonderful opportunities or met wonderful people. The problem is, we haven't known how to take the greatest advantage of the opportunities we've had. Sometimes we didn't recognize at the time how wonderful those people were. Love is all around us. The ego is the block to our awareness of love's presence. The idea that there is a perfect person who just hasn't arrived yet is a major block.

Our vulnerability to the myth of "Mr. Right" stems from our glorification of romantic love. The ego uses romantic love for its "special" purposes, leading us to jeopardize our relationships by overvaluing their romantic content. The difference between a friendship and a romance can be illustrated with the image of a long-stemmed rose. The stem is the friendship; the blossom the romance. Because the ego is sensation-oriented, our focus automatically goes to the blossom. But all the nourishment that the blossom needs in order to live, reaches it through the stem. The stem might look boring in comparison, but if you take the blossom off the stem it will not last for long. I shared that image in a lecture once, and a woman then added a lovely thought: A long-term romance is like a rose bush. In any given season, a blossom might fall off. But if the plant is well nourished, then the season will come around again, and new blossoms appear. The disappearance of romantic fervor doesn't necessarily spell the end of a wonderful relationship, except to the ego. The Spirit can see the seeds of rebirth in any pattern of decline.

A Course in Miracles says it is not our job to seek for love, but to seek for all the barriers we hold against its coming. Thinking that there is some special person out there who is going to save us is a barrier to pure love. It is a large gun in the ego's arsenal. It is a way the ego tries to keep us away from love, although it doesn't want us to see that. We seek desperately for love, but it is that same desperation that leads us to destroy it once it gets here. Thinking that one special person is going to save us tempts us to load an awful lot of emotional pressure on whoever comes along that we think might fit the bill.

We don't have to remind God that we'd like wonderful relationships. He's already clear about that. *A Course in Miracles* teaches us that a desire is a prayer. The most enlightened prayer isn't "Dear God, send me someone wonderful," but, "Dear God, help me realize that I am someone wonderful." Years ago I would pray for a wonderful man to come and take my desperation away. Ultimately I said to myself, "Why don't you try to deal with that before he gets here?" I can't imagine any man saying to a friend, "Gee, I met a fabulous desperate woman last night!" Looking for Mr. Right leads to desperation because there is no Mr. Right. There is no Mr. Right because there is no Mr. Wrong. There is whoever is in front of us, and the perfect lessons to be learned from that person.

If your heart's desire is for an intimate partner, the Holy Spirit might send someone who isn't the ultimate intimate partner for you, but rather something better: someone with whom you are given the opportunity to work through the places in yourself that need to be healed before you're *ready* for the deepest intimacy. The belief in special love leads us to discount anything we don't see as "ultimate relationship" material. I've overlooked some diamonds that way, failing to take advantage of situations that would have only served to speed up my growth. We sometimes fail to work on ourselves in the relationships that are right in front of us, thinking that "real life" begins when *they* get here. This is just a ploy of the ego once again, making sure that we'll seek but not find. The problem with not taking relationships seriously if they don't feel like "Mr. Right" is this: Every once in a while, Mr. Right gets here—he sometimes even appears as Mr. Wrong transformed—but we blow it because we're not in practice. He's here, but we're not ready. We haven't been working on ourselves. We were waiting for Mr. Right.

A Course in Miracles says that one day we will realize that nothing occurs outside our minds. How a person seems to show up for us is intimately connected to how we choose to show up for them. I have learned that my most productive responses in relationships come not from my focus on the particulars about another person, but rather from my commitment to playing my own role in the relationship on as high a level as I'm capable. Love is a participatory emotion. In a holy relationship, we take an active role in creating the context in which the interaction can unfold most constructively. We actively create the conditions of interest, rather than passively waiting around to see whether or not we're interested.

No one is always gorgeous. No one is always sexy. But love is a decision. Waiting to see whether someone is good enough is childish, and it is bound to make the other person feel on some level as though they're auditioning for the part. In that space, we feel nervous, and when we're nervous, we're not at our best. The ego is looking for someone attractive enough to support. The mature and miracle-minded among us support people in being attractive. Part of working on ourselves, in order to be ready for a profound relationship, is learning how to support another person in being the best that they can be. Partners are meant to have a priestly role in each other's lives. They are meant to help each other access the highest parts within themselves.

I've been with men who never seemed to think I

was good enough. I've also been with men who were smart enough to say, "You look beautiful tonight" often enough for it to bolster my self-esteem and help me show up for life in a more beautiful way. None of us are really objectively attractive or unattractive. There is no such thing. There are people who manifest the potential for sparkle that we all share, and those who don't. Those who do are usually people who somewhere along the line, either from parents or lovers, were told verbally or nonverbally, "You're wonderful and beautiful." Love is to people what water is to plants.

Examining the past can help clarify many of our problems, but healing doesn't occur in the past. It occurs in the present. There is practically a mania these days for blaming the events of our childhood for our current despair. What the ego doesn't want us to see is that our pain doesn't come from the love we weren't given in the past, but from the love we ourselves aren't giving in the present. Salvation is only found in the present. Every moment we have a chance to change our past and our future by reprogramming the present. Such a view is blasphemy to the ego and we are judged harshly for espousing it. Although we might have learned the ways of lovelessness from our parents, perpetuating their patterns by denying them love now is hardly the way out of the problem. We don't get to the light through endless investigation of the darkness. After a certain point, the discussion always becomes circular. The only way to the light is through entering the light.

"My parents didn't tell me I was beautiful. Poor me." is not a miracle-minded thought. Rather, it supports a feeling of victimization. The miracle-minded attitude here would be, "My parents didn't tell me I was beautiful. The value of knowing this is that now I'm clearer about why I don't have an easy time letting anyone else tell me that, and I understand why I haven't developed the habit of saying it to others. I can develop the habit now. The choice to give what I haven't received is always an available option." A man mentioned to me recently that when he was a child, his father never gave him presents. I suggested that a healing would come from his sending his father lots of presents now.

I used to worry too much about whether or not I was supported, and not enough about whether or not I was actively supporting others. Romantically, I realized that I needed to help a man feel more like a man, rather than spend my time worrying about whether or not he *was* enough of a man. We help another person access their highest by accessing our own. Growth comes from focus on our own lessons, not on someone else's. *A Course in Miracles* teaches that "only what you have not given can be lacking in any situation." I spent years waiting for a man to make me "feel like a real woman." Only when I realized that my feminine energy was not a man's gift to me, but rather my gift to myself and to him, did the men around me start to demonstrate the more masculine energy I craved.

The fairy tale called "The Frog Prince" reveals the

deep psychological connection between our attitudes toward people and their capacity for transformation. In the story, a princess kisses a frog and he becomes a prince. What this signifies is the miraculous power of love to create a context in which people naturally blossom into their highest potential. Neither nagging, trying to get people to change, criticizing, or fixing can do that. The Course says we think we're going to understand people in order to figure out whether or not they're worthy of our love, but that actually, until we love them, we can never understand them. What is not loved is not understood. We hold ourselves separate from people and wait for them to earn our love. But people deserve our love because of what God created them to be. As long as we're waiting for them to be anything better, we will constantly be disappointed. When we choose to join with them, through approval and unconditional love, the miracle kicks in for both parties. This is the primary key, the ultimate miracle, in relationships.

9.   RELINQUISHING FEAR

"Perfect love casts out fear."

A good relationship isn't always crystals and rainbows. It's a birth process, often painful, often messy. When my daughter was first born, she was covered with blood and everything else. There was a lot to go through before the Gerber baby finally appeared.

A "spiritual relationship" isn't necessarily one in which two people are smiling all the time. Spiritual means to me, above all else, authentic. At my New Year's Eve service last year, I said that we were together not for mindless but for mindful celebration. That would include some grief and acknowledgement of disappointments in the past year, which would have to be processed and forgiven before we could honestly celebrate the stroke of midnight and the mark of a new beginning.

And so it is that, in relationships as well, we're brought together for real work. Real work can only occur in the presence of rigorous honesty. We all long for that, but we are afraid of honestly communicating with another person because we think they'll leave us if they see who we really are.

A couple from my lectures once came to me for counseling. Earlier that day, the man had told the woman he was breaking off their relationship. She was shocked and hurt and asked him if he would come with her to see me in order to help her work through the loss. As the two of them sat across from me on my couch, I assured Bob that I wasn't there to try to get them back together, but to join with them in asking for peace.

I remembered a similar situation I had been in myself once, and how brilliantly my therapist had handled it. I said exactly the things that she had said. I said to him, "Bob, why are you so angry at Deborah?"

"I'm not angry at her," he said.

"Well, you sure sound angry," I told him.

"I know that it's not my job to fix Deborah," he said. "I don't want to change her; I just want out."

"Oh, I bet you think that's so spiritual," I said.

He looked surprised. I think he thought he'd been a good *A Course in Miracles* student.

"You haven't suspended judgment of Deborah," I said. "You've withheld vital information from her, data without which she couldn't function effectively within the relationship. Why don't you tell her why you're so angry?"

Once again he repeated, "I'm not angry."

"Well," I said. "You're an actor. Just pretend you are. Go on Bob, we're safe here. Let her have it."

And boy, once he got started, did he let it out. He told her that she had no concept of how to live with another person. She just did everything however she wanted to do it, and if he wanted to come along, well that was just great. I don't remember exactly what else he had to say, but there was a lot of communication that came gushing out once he allowed it to. When he was finished, Deborah, obviously moved, said quietly and sincerely, "I never knew that. Thank you for telling me."

They left my office and did not break up. Their relationship, they later told me, was reborn in that session. The anger that Bob was feeling was pent up energy that came from the fact that he had felt it "unspiritual" to share his honest feelings with Deborah as they went along.

It's far better to communicate than to suppress our feelings. Anger is often a result of a series of uncommunicated feelings building up inside of us and ultimately exploding. In a holy relationship, we consider it part of our commitment to stay current in the honest expression of our feelings, and to support our partner in doing the same. So much is then communicated as we go along that the chances of anger building up inside either of us is lessened.

Until then, we must deal with what's real. If anger comes up, it must be accepted. If we think our partner won't love us if we get angry, then we stop being honest and the relationship is doomed for sure. I've suggested to couples that they agree not to break up a relationship because of a fight. It's very important to have a safe space for fighting. I say that because fighting isn't always fighting. Once I was having a "dramatic discussion" with a friend. A mutual friend of ours spoke up and said, "I can't stand the way you guys are always fighting." "We're not fighting," I said. "We're Jewish." He thought we were fighting; we thought we were having a passionate conversation.

Anger is a hot topic for spiritual seekers. Many people, for instance, have an issue with Jesus's anger with the money-changers. If Jesus was so pure, they ask, then how could he have gotten angry? But no Jew or Italian would have a problem with that scene. The removal of ego is not the removal of personality. What we call Jesus's anger was energy. An outburst of emotion doesn't have to be so quickly labeled anger. It's a release of energy and doesn't have to be thought of as a negative or "unspiritual" emotion.

Just because someone isn't expressing their rage, by the way, doesn't mean they don't have any. Rage turned outward is called rage. Rage turned inward is called ulcers and cancer and things like that. The unhealthiest thing you can do with anger is to deny you have it. The miraculous perspective is not to pretend you're not angry, but rather to say, "I'm angry but I'm willing not to be. Dear God, please show me what it is I'm not seeing." There is a way of sharing our anger with people, without expressing it as an attack. Instead of saying, for instance, "You made me feel this or that," you say, "This is how I'm feeling. I'm not saying *you made me feel* this way, or that you're to blame. I'm simply sharing this as part of my healing, in order to release this feeling and move beyond it." In this way, you're taking responsibility for your feelings, and what could have been seen as an argument—or even avoided as unpleasant—can become an important part of the healing power of relationships. We're then not adversaries in the conversation, but partners. Real relationships demand honest communication, no matter how painful, no matter how frightening. *A Course in Miracles* says that miracles arise from total communication given and received.

When you ask God to heal your life, He shines a very bright light on everything you need to look at. You end up seeing things about yourself that maybe you'd rather not see. We have a lot of armor that has accumulated in front of our hearts—a lot of fear self-righteously masquerading as something else. As anyone who has ever been in serious psychotherapy is well aware, the process of personal growth isn't always easy. We must face our own ugliness. We often must become painfully aware of the unworkability of a pattern before we're willing to give it up. It often seems, in fact, that our lives get worse rather than better when we begin to work deeply on ourselves. Life doesn't actually get worse; it's just that we feel our own transgressions more because we're no longer anesthetized by unconsciousness. We're no longer distanced, through denial or dissociation, from our own experience. We're starting to see the truth about the games we play.

This process can be so painful that we are tempted to go backwards. It takes courage—this is often called the path of the spiritual warrior—to endure the sharp pains of self-discovery rather than choose to take the dull pain of unconsciousness that would last the rest of our lives. I laugh whenever anyone suggests that *A Course in Miracles* has us taking an easy way out. It's a lot of things, but it's *not* easy. We have to look the ego straight in the eye before we have the power to relinquish it.

The ego isn't a monster. It's just the *idea* of a monster. We all have demons and dragons within us, but we also have the dashing prince. I've never read a fairy tale where the dragons triumphed over the prince. And I've never really tried to outgrow a pattern and not had the experience of God's grace given me when I sincerely and humbly asked. "You take the good with the bad," my father used to tell us when we were children. The more we learn about the light within us, the easier it ultimately becomes to forgive ourselves for the fact that we're not perfect yet. If we were perfect, we wouldn't have been born. It's our mission to become perfect, however, and looking at where we're not is an important part of the process. We become perfected personalities by accepting the spiritual perfection which already exists within us.

There is a story about Leonardo da Vinci that has always moved me. Early in his career, he was painting a picture of Christ and found a profoundly beautiful young male to model for his portrait of Jesus. Many years later, Leonardo was painting a picture that included Judas. He walked through the streets of Florence looking for the perfect person to play the great betrayer. Finally he found someone dark-looking enough, evil-seeming enough to do the job. He went up to the man to approach him to do the modeling. The man looked at him and said, "You don't remember me, but I know you. Years ago, I was the model for your picture of Jesus."

In the movie *Star Wars*, Darth Vader turns out to have been a nice guy after all, a long time ago. And Lucifer was the most beautiful angel in Heaven before he fell. The ego is simply where a glitch occurred, where the wires got crossed, where love became blocked. As many times as I've expressed negativity instead of love in my life, there's one thing I'm very sure of: I would have done better if I had known how. I would have expressed with love if I had felt at that moment that I could have, and still had my needs met.

Until we fully appreciate that the ego is the impostor within us, we often feel embarrassed to admit to ourselves, not to mention anyone else, the games we play. Instead of feeling compassion for ourselves, and remembering that our neuroses are our wounds, we tend to be too ashamed to look at them. We think we're bad. We think that if we, or anyone else God forbid, were to see the real truth about us, we would all recoil in horror. The truth, rather, is that if we, or anyone else, were to see the real truth about us, we would all be dazzled by the light. In looking deeply into ourselves, however, we first have to face what *A Course in Miracles* calls the ring of fear. Before the Prince can save the damsel in distress, he has to slay the dragons that surround her castle. So do we all. Those dragons are our demons, our wounds, our egos, our brilliant ways of denying love to ourselves and others. The ego's patterns have to be rooted out, detoxed from our system, before the pure love within us can have a chance to come forth.

A spiritual teacher from India once pointed out that there is no such thing as a gray sky. The sky is always blue. Sometimes, however, gray clouds come and cover the blue sky. We then think the sky is gray. It is the same with our minds. We're always perfect. We can't not be. Our fearful patterns, our dysfunctional habits, take hold within our minds and cover our perfection. Temporarily.

That is all. We are still perfect sons of God. There has never been a storm that hasn't passed. Gray clouds never last forever. The blue sky does.

So what are we to do with our fear, our anger, the clouds that cover the love inside us? Relinquish them to the Holy Spirit. He transforms them through love, and never through an attack on another person. It is attack, not the anger itself, which is destructive. Yelling into pillows has become popular in certain circles, and for good reason. Getting the energy up and out is often a good way to shed the physical tension that makes it so difficult to pray when you need it most. Our anger stands in front of our love. Letting it out is part of the process of relinquishing it. The last thing you want to do—ever—is to buy into the insidious delusion that spiritual lives and spiritual relationships are always quiet, or always blissful.

10.   WORKING ON OURSELVES

"Only what you have not given can be lacking in any situation."

Relationships are meaningful because they are opportunities to expand our hearts and become more deeply loving. The Holy Spirit is the medium of miracles, a guide to a different way of viewing ourselves in relation to other people. I watch my baby as she extends her love to everyone she meets. She hasn't learned yet that anyone is unsafe. Nothing stands between her natural impulse to love and her expression of that love. She smiles with the tenderness of her true feelings. One day I will have to teach her that not every expression of love is appropriate. But locking your door is vastly different from locking your heart. The greatest challenge of parenthood will be to support her in keeping an open heart while living in such a fearful world.

We can't really give to our children what we don't have ourselves. In that sense, my greatest gift to my daughter is that I continue to work on myself. Children learn more through imitation than through any other form of instruction. Our greatest opportunity to positively affect another person's life is to accept God's love into our own.

That is one of the primary principles of miracles in relationships: We are to look to ourselves—our own lessons, thoughts and behavior—in order to find peace with another person. "The sole responsibility of the miracleworker is to accept the Atonement for himself." The ego will always tempt us to think that the breakdown of a relationship has to do with what *they* did wrong, or what *they're* not seeing, or what *they* need to learn. The focus must remain on ourselves. We're affected by other peoples' lovelessness only to the extent to which we judge them for it. Otherwise we are invulnerable to the ego, as the Son of God is meant to be.

Sometimes people will say to me, "But Marianne, I think ninety percent of this is their stuff." "Fine," I say. "Then we have ten percent to investigate and learn from." That ten percent that is "your" part is what you need to look at and learn from. It is what you will carry with you into the next scenario. The ego knows this, which is why it tries to put the focus on the other person. The ego's purpose is to make us continually self-destruct without knowing that we're doing it. It's hard enough cleaning up your own act. Trying to clean up someone else's is just an ego trick to keep you from applying yourself to your own lessons. In order to learn the most from relationships, you have to focus on your own issues.

These days it's very common to hear people complain that their issue is that they choose the "wrong" people. The ego is very sly here. It's trying to convince us that we're taking responsibility for the problem, when in fact we're only doing that to a very small degree. Because our description of the problem still makes someone guilty, it can only lead into further darkness, not light. "I continue to choose people who can't commit" is not a miracle-minded perception. A more enlightened question might be, "How committable am I, really? How prepared am I in the deepest recesses of my being to give and receive love in an intimate, committed way?" Or, "How can I forgive those who could not go past a certain wall of fear when dealing with me? How can I forgive myself for the ways in which I contributed to or participated in their fear?"

Sometimes it seems as though you're hooked: You feel obsessed or compulsive about another person. When this is the case, it's a pretty good bet that on some level you're not letting them off the hook. In spite of the temptation to look outside yourself for the source as well as the answer to a problem, you hold to miracle-minded thought by looking inside yourself for both. The price you pay for not taking responsibility for your own pain is the failure to realize that you can change your conditions by changing your thoughts. Regardless of who initiated a painful interaction, or how much of the error still lies in someone else's thinking, the Holy Spirit always provides you with complete escape from pain through forgiveness on your part. The other person doesn't have to consciously join you in the change. Whoever is saner at the time, says *A Course in Miracles*, is to invite the Holy Spirit into a situation. It doesn't matter whether or not another person shares our willingness to let God enter. Everything you need in life already exists inside your head.

I once had a crush on a gay man. It might have been unreasonable, but I couldn't get him out of my mind. I asked for a miracle, and the following thoughts occurred to me: "You know, Marianne, you're obsessed, you're so unreleased about this because you're not releasing *him*. Accept him as he is. Release him to be where he wants to be, doing whatever he wants to do with whomever he wants to do it. It's what *you're* not giving that is lacking here. It's what *you're* doing to *him* that's causing you pain. Emotionally, your ego is trying to control him, which is why you're feeling controlled by your emotions." I got it. I released him in my mind, and then I felt released.

11. CLOSED HEARTS

"No one can doubt the ego's skill in building up false cases."

I once knew a man who came on very strong at the beginning of relationships, but couldn't seem to help closing his heart as soon as a woman had opened hers. I have heard that kind of behavior referred to as an "addiction to the attraction phase" in relationships. This man did not maliciously go around hurting women. He sincerely wanted to be in a genuine, committed relationship. What he lacked were the spiritual skills that would enable him to settle down in one place long enough to build anything solid with an equal partner. As soon as he saw human faults and weaknesses in a woman, he would run. The narcissistic personality is looking for perfection, which is a way of making sure that love never has a chance to blossom. The initial high can be so heady, so tantalizing, that the real work of growth which needs to follow the initial attraction phase can seem too dull, too hard to commit to. As soon as the other person is seen to be a real human being, the ego is repelled and wants to find somewhere else to play.

At the end of a relationship with someone like this, we feel as though we've taken cocaine. We had a fast and very exciting ride, and it felt at the time like something meaningful was happening. Then we crashed and realized that nothing meaningful had happened at all. It was all made up. Now all we have is a headache, and we can see that this kind of thing isn't good, isn't healthy, and we don't want to do it again.

But there's a reason why we're attracted to relationships such as this. We were drawn to the illusion of meaning. Sometimes someone who has nothing to offer in a real relationship can come on like they're offering the world. They are so dissociated from their own feelings that they have become highly skilled performers, unconsciously playing whatever part our fantasies prescribe. But the responsibility for our pain still remains our own. If we hadn't been looking for a cheap thrill, we wouldn't have been vulnerable to the lie.

How could we have been so stupid? That's the question we always ask ourselves at the end of these experiences. But once we've had enough of them, we admit to ourselves that we weren't really stupid at all. We suspected this was a drug. The problem was, we wanted it. We saw exactly what the game was with this person, usually within the first fifteen minutes, yet we were so attracted to the high, we were willing to pretend we didn't see it, for just a night, or a week, or however long it lasted. The fact that someone said to us, "You are so fabulous. You're such a wonderful woman. This is such a great date. How lucky a guy is to get to date you," when he's only known you for an hour, is a blinking red light to any thinking woman. The problem is, the depth of our wounds can be so great—we can be so hungry to hear those words, because deep down we suspect that they're untrue—that hearing them can cause us to put aside all rational considerations. When we're starved, we're desperate.

Women say to me sometimes, "Marianne, why do I always meet emotionally abusive men?" My answer is usually the following: "The problem is not that you met him—the problem is that you gave him your number." The problem, in other words, is not that we attract a certain kind of person, but rather that we are attracted *to* a certain kind of person. Someone who is distant emotionally might remind us, for instance, of one or both of our parents. "His energy is distant and subtly disapproving—I must be home." The problem, then, is not just that we are offered pain, but that we are *comfortable* with that pain. It's what we have always known.

The flip side of our dangerous attractions to people who have nothing to offer us is our tendency to feel bored by people who do. Nothing that is alien to our system can enter into us and stay there for long. This is true whether we're talking about something taken into our bodies or into our minds. If I swallow a piece of aluminum foil, my body will regurgitate until the offending object is expelled. If I'm being asked to swallow an idea that doesn't "agree" with me, then my psychological system will go through the same process of regurgitation in order to expel the offending material.

If I'm convinced that I'm not good enough, I will have a difficult time accepting someone into my life who thinks I am. It's the Groucho Marx syndrome of not wanting to like anyone who would want me in their club. The only way that I can accept someone's finding me wonderful, is if I find myself wonderful. But to the ego, self-acceptance is death.

This is why we're attracted to people who don't want us. We know they're not into it from the gate. We pretend to be surprised later when we find ourselves betrayed and they leave after an intense but fairly short stay. They fit perfectly into our ego's plan: I will not be loved. The reason that nice, available people seem boring to us is because they bust us. The ego equates emotional danger with excitement, and claims that the nice, available person isn't dangerous enough. The irony is that the opposite is true: available people are the ones who *are* dangerous, because they confront us with the possibility of real intimacy. They might actually hang around long enough to get to know us. They could melt our defenses, not through violence but through love. This is what the ego doesn't want us to see. Available people are frightening. They threaten the ego's citadel. The reason we're not attracted to them is because we're not available ourselves.

12.   HEALING OUR WOUNDS

"Healing is the way in which separation is overcome."

Our barriers to love are rarely consciously chosen. They are our efforts to protect the places where the heart is bruised. Somewhere, sometime, we felt as though an open heart caused us pain or humiliation. We loved with the openness of a child, and someone didn't care, or laughed, or even punished us for the effort. In a quick moment, perhaps a fraction of a second, we made a decision to protect ourselves from ever feeling that pain again. We would never again allow ourselves to be so vulnerable. We built emotional defenses. We tried to build a fortress across our heart, to protect us from any cold assault. The only problem is, according to the Course, that we create what we defend against.

There was a time in my life when I felt I should stop opening up so much to people who didn't honor my heart as I wished it to be honored. I was angry at people who I felt had hurt me, but I denied the anger instead of getting in touch with it and releasing it to God. This is a common trap for Course students. If anger isn't brought up into conscious awareness, it has no place to go. It either turns into an attack on self or an inappropriate unconscious attack on others.

So not recognizing the full extent of my anger, and thinking that the lesson to be learned was merely that I shouldn't reveal so much of my honest feelings, I then went into relationships with two strikes against me: I was closed—read that as cold—and armed with hidden emotional knives coming from my unconscious anger. Contrary to whatever front I might have been able to lead with, that's not exactly a delightful package. Between the coldness and the anger, I could turn off the saintliest men. This, of course, only increased my anger and distrust.

I was once talking to a very wise therapist. I made some comment like, "Well, a lot of women my age are finding it very hard to find really loving, committable, available men." Her answer rang through my head like church bells. "When a woman says that to me," she said, "what we usually find when we look closely enough is a contempt for men."

Contempt for men. Contempt for men. The words resounded through my skull. I don't know if that was the issue for every woman she spoke to, but I knew she had hit the nail on the head in my case. I had often thought about the idea in the Course that we think we are angry at what our brother did to us, but that really we are angry because of what we've done to him. I had vaguely known that that was true, but it took a lot of uncovering to see what it was I was *doing* to these guys who I just *knew* were doing all these horrible things to me! The Course speaks of "shadow figures" we bring with us from our past. It tells us that we tend to see no one as they are now. We keep blaming someone in the present for something someone else did in the past. Some poor man would tell me, "Darling, I'm not able to come back Sunday night like I'd planned. I've got to keep working on this project. I might not be back until Tuesday." Well, he might as well have just told me that my cat was dead and the dog was dying. The problem wasn't that the man wasn't coming home for a few days more. The problem was how it made me feel inside to hear him say that. Such a dark despair would run across my heart, I can't begin to tell you. I wasn't relating to that man, or this circumstance. I was remembering all the times I had ever felt as though I didn't matter, I wasn't attractive, Daddy didn't want to hold me, or someone else didn't want to have sex anymore.

From a Course perspective, this situation was coming up now in order for me to feel that feeling, and know that it had nothing to do with the present. I asked for a miracle: I am willing to see this differently. I am willing to remember who I am. God's answer to my pain was not going to be—contrary to what my ego kept insisting was the only way out of this grief—a man who was going to tell me sixty times a day, "You're fabulous, you're wonderful, I love you, I want you," and then show me just how desirable I really was, maybe twice, preferably three times a day. The healing, in fact, was bound to come ultimately from men who would not—because no one can, really—tolerate my neediness, or the guilt I would try to project onto them in order to get my needs met. Or what I thought my needs were. My real need, of course, was to realize that I didn't need a man to fill what only felt like these insatiable emotional needs. The needs themselves were not real, but merely a reflection of the fact that I thought of myself as less than perfect. Salvation would only come through my relinquishing the thought that I wasn't good enough. By defending myself against being abandoned, I continued to recreate the conditions in which it was bound to occur.

Why can't men commit? I can only answer for some of them that I've known, but in those cases, and in the cases of many women I've observed, men haven't committed because the women have been armored against it. Our armor is our darkness—the dark of the heart, the dark of the pain, the dark of the moment when we make that wicked comment or that unfair request.

Our defenses reflect our wounds. But no person can heal those wounds. They can give us love, innocently and sincerely, but if we're already convinced that people can't be trusted—if that's the decision we've already made—then our mind will construe whatever someone's behavior is, as evidence that our previously drawn conclusion was correct. The Course tells us we decide what we want to see before we see it. If we want to focus on someone's lack of respect for our feelings, we can certainly find it, given the fact that I don't know of many enlightened masters available for dating in the major cities of America today. But a lot of people are making greater efforts than we give them credit for, and are working against some formidable odds when our egos have convinced us that men or women are jerks, or don't like us, or always leave, or that there just aren't any good ones out there.

13.   CHANGING OUR MIND

"The fundamental change will occur with the change of mind in the thinker."

The goal of spiritual practice is full recovery, and the only thing you need to recover from is a fractured sense of self. If you don't already believe it yourself, another person cannot convince you you're okay. If they act as though you are, you will either not believe them, or become so dependent on their reinforcement that you proceed through your dependency to change their mind. Either way, you stay convinced that you're not okay. The only exercise in the Workbook of *A Course in Miracles* that is repeated several times is "I am as God created me." As I have mentioned earlier, the Course says that your only real problem is that you have forgotten who you are.

You awaken to your own perfection through your desire to see the perfection in someone else. Sometimes this is not easy. When I feel the old familiar darkness starting to descend around me, when a man, for instance, makes a comment that I know intellectually is probably innocent enough, but which makes me feel that I am abandoned or uncared for or rejected, I've been through enough in my life to know that the evil does not lie in what he just said. He is not the enemy. The enemy is this feeling, which in the past has led me to attack or defend enough to make him feel exactly what I'm feeling he's feeling but he really isn't. I can choose to see this differently. This is my wall. This is where we must be very conscious and call on God. Ask for a miracle: "Dear God, please help me. This is it. Right here. There is where the sword enters my heart. This is where I blow it every time."

The moment when the pain is greatest is a wonderful opportunity. The ego would prefer that we never look too directly into the pain. When in crisis, there's a good opportunity we might have a slip and ask Heaven for help. The ego would prefer that we not go into crisis. The ego prefers that a mild river of misery run through the background of our lives, never bad enough to make us question whether our own choices are creating the pain. When the pain is here, that is when we have a chance to "rout Satan and remove him forever." A man once said to me, "You know, Marianne, you can work on this stuff with your therapist, *A Course in Miracles*, your editor, the relationships lecturer, and all of your girlfriends, but none of them provide you with the opportunity that you have by working it out with me." What he meant of course, is with them I could describe the pain, but with him I could feel it. And in that moment, if I didn't take the childish, narcissistic copout and leave, but remained to face the fear and move through it, then the purpose of the relationship could be fulfilled. When our darkness is brought to light and forgiven, then we can move on.

We heal through noticing, and prayer. Awareness

alone does not heal us. If analysis by itself could heal our wounds, we would all be healed by now. Our neuroses have become deeply embedded into our psyches, like a tumor that wraps itself around a vital organ.

The process of miraculous change is twofold:

1. I see my error or dysfunctional pattern.
2. I ask God to take it from me.

The first principle without the second is impotent. As they say in Alcoholics Anonymous, "your best thinking got you here." You're the problem but you're not the answer.

The second principle isn't enough to change us, either. The Holy Spirit can't take from us what we won't release to Him. He won't work without our consent. He cannot remove our character defects without our willingness, because that would be violating our free will. We chose those patterns, however mistakenly, and He will not force us to give them up.

In asking God to heal you, you are committing to the choice to be healed. This means the choice to change. The ego's resistance to this is intense. It wants us to think that an old dog doesn't change. "I'm angry because I'm an alcoholic," for instance, might describe your anger, but it doesn't justify it. The only advantage of knowing that you're angry, is so that you can make a choice to be otherwise. You can spend years in therapy, but until the choice is made to *do it differently*, you just keep going around in circles. Of course it feels unnatural to be gentle when you've been harsh for many years, but that's no excuse for not trying.

A Course in Miracles says that the most effective way to teach a child is not by saying "Don't do that" but "Do this." We don't reach the light through endless analysis of the dark. We reach the light by choosing the light. Light means understanding. Through understanding, we are healed.

If the purpose of a relationship is for people to be healed, and healing can only occur when our wounds are revealed, then the ego confronts us with a terrible Catch-22. If I don't show myself, there can be no growth. Without growth, there will ultimately be boredom, which is death for the relationship. But if I do reveal myself honestly, then I might appear unattractive and my partner will leave.

The ego's narcissism has us waiting for the perfect person to appear. The Holy Spirit knows that the search for perfection in another is just a smokescreen that hides our need to develop the perfect within ourselves. And if there is a perfect person out there—which there isn't— would they date *you*? When we give up the childish obsession with scanning the planet for Mr. or Ms. Right, we can begin to develop the skills of compassionate relationship. We stop judging people and start relating to them instead. We recognize, first and foremost, that we're not in a relationship to focus on how well the other person is learning their lessons, but rather to focus on learning our own.

The ego defends against love, not fear. Pain in relationships can be a perversely comfortable pain, in that it is one we know. We're used to it. I once heard a tape by Ram Dass, an American spiritual teacher, in which he told of seeing a newspaper article about an abused baby being taken away from his mother. As a police matron tried to take the baby, he kept struggling to remain in his mother's arms. Although his mother was the one who beat him, she was the one he knew. He was used to her. He wanted to remain in familiar territory.

This story illustrates our relationship to our own egos. The ego is our pain, but it is what we know, and we resist moving out of it. The effort it takes to grow out of painful patterns often feels more uncomfortable than remaining within them. Personal growth can be painful, because it can make us feel ashamed and humiliated to face our own darkness. But the goal of personal growth is the journey out of dark emotional patterns that cause us pain, to those that create peace. *Psychotherapy: Purpose, Process and Practice* says that at their peak, religion and psychotherapy become one. They both represent the relationship between thought and experience, and are used by the Holy Spirit to celebrate one of the most glorious human potentials: our capacity to change.

There is a tendency these days to analyze our neuroses ad infinitum, yet use the analysis itself to justify rather than heal the wound. After a certain point, having seen why a pattern developed ("My father was emotionally unavailable," or "My mother abused me") and the effect it has had on our personalities ("I don't know how to let a man get close to me," or "I now have a hard time trusting any authority figure"), actual change occurs because of a decision on our part: the decision to heal, the decision to change. It ultimately doesn't matter so much why I become angry or defensive. What matters is that I decide I want to be healed, and I ask God to help me.

Like an actor reading lines from a script, I can choose a new response to life, a new reading. Some people at this point would yell, "Denial!" But what we are denying is the impostor within us. Just because we have an honest feeling, that doesn't mean it's who we honestly are. My angry self is *not* the real me. Does it have to be acknowledged? Yes, but only in order to go beyond it. Once I've seen my anger, I'm ready, as they say in AA, to "act as if" I can do it differently. Because I can. Our ego has made up a fictional character that we now think of as our personality. But we are constantly creating that personality, and if we choose, we are constantly recreating it.

I was once talking to a friend and he made some comment about how he was afraid that, if we got closely involved, one of us might get hurt. "Which one of us are you concerned for?" I asked. He answered, "You."

I felt an anticipatory rejection. I was angry and I told him so.

"That's what I mean," he said. "You obviously take things so personally that I don't think I could stand it for long."

I knew that this was a moment I had repeated in various ways with various people, and I had asked for healing many times. I was open. I asked him, "Tell me honestly: How could I have done it differently? What else could I have said?"

"You could have just smiled and said, 'Don't flatter yourself.'"

I was so excited. I was like an eager actress working with a great director. "Oh that's so great," I said. "Let's go back and do that scene one more time. Say what you said again."

"You know, Marianne, I just have this awful feeling that if we really got together, one of us would get hurt."

"Which one of us are you afraid for?" I asked.

"You."

I looked at him and smiled. "Don't flatter yourself."

He laughed and I howled with excitement. This had been no small awakening. It was a genuine empowerment, a reprogramming of my emotional computer in an area where I had unconsciously gone for an unworkable response pattern every time. I now established a new groove, a new set of possibilities. Initially I had chosen the way of anger. Now I chose the way of love. I did not have to be the wounded animal. I could choose to identify with my own strength, which was in fact the more natural role for me to play. I could choose to see others through a generous, trusting nature. My brother was not here to attack me. He was here to love me. It was completely up to me whether to trust that, and love him back.

In accepting the Atonement, the correction of our perceptions, we are returned to who we really are. Our true, purely loving self can never be uncreated. All illusions will be undone. Although experiences such as childhood trauma can lead us to deviate from our true nature, the truth itself is held in trust for us by the Holy Spirit until we choose to return.

14.   PRACTICING FORGIVENESS

"Forgiveness is the only sane response."

To the ego, love is a crime. It seeks to convince us that forgiveness is a dangerous position that entails an unfair sacrifice on our part. The ego claims that forgiveness can lead us into situations where we become someone's doormat. To the ego, love is weakness. To the Holy Spirit, love is strength.

I was dating someone several years ago when the Olympic games were playing in Los Angeles. The opening ceremonies were a marvelous theatrical presentation and it was very difficult to get tickets. Because he was involved in the media, Mike was given, at the last minute, one pass that would enable him to go.

I was very excited for him. Everyone in town knew it was going to be a wonderful event. We decided that I would watch the ceremonies on T.V. and we would meet afterwards. At the conclusion of the broadcast, I started getting dressed and figured that it might be an hour or so before I heard from him, since the traffic around the stadium was bound to be horrendous.

An hour passed and then another. Well, he's in T.V., I thought, so maybe something came up. Another hour and then another. Midnight came and went. I took off my clothes and make-up. It was 2 A.M., then 3. At times I fell asleep, at times I lay in the dark and stared at the ceiling, at times I was livid, and at other times I was scared he was lying in a ditch somewhere. I started calling his house. No answer. I'd call again. No answer. Finally, hardly having slept at all, I called at around 6 A.M. and he answered the phone.

"Hello," he said.

"Mike?" I said. "This is Marianne."

"Oh, hi."

"Are you all right?"

"Yeah, why?"

"We had a date yesterday. Did you forget?"

"Oh, right," he said. "I had a kind of late night."

I don't know what I said to get off the phone, but I know how I felt and it wasn't wonderful. I had been stood up and I felt the kind of blow to my self-esteem that starts in your gut and shoots emotional black ink through all your veins. Dazed, I somehow fell asleep.

When I woke up, I had a whole new take on the situation. I just knew that he was going to wake up feeling sorry for how he had acted. He was going to show up at my door any minute, carrying a dozen roses and saying, "Hi, babe, can I take you to brunch?" The scenario in my head called for my being oh-so-gracious: "Of course you can, darling" would come out of my mouth in a girlish melody. The problem is, he never came. Not only did he not come. He never called.

I was in a dark zone. Now what would *A Course in Miracles* say about that? I knew I needed a miracle. But all I could come up with were two choices for ways to deal with this, both of which I had tried before in similar situations, and neither one felt good or got me what I wanted.

My first choice was to get very angry and let him know it. "Who do you think you are to treat me like that, you son-of-a-bitch?" The problem with that choice was that it would completely invalidate my position. "Marianne's a nice girl, but her temper just doesn't cut it. She's hysterical when she doesn't get her way."

The only other choice I could imagine was to forgive him and let it go. But that didn't feel good either. "It's okay you stood me up, Mike. I don't care. It doesn't matter." Unconditional love I could understand, but not unconditional dating. I didn't know what to do. I asked for a miracle. I considered the possibility of another possibility. I gave the situation to God and remembered that I need do nothing.

From a Course perspective, the first thing I had to deal with was my own judgment. As long as I was not at peace, my behavior would carry the energy of my conflict. Conflicted behavior cannot bring peace. It can only produce more conflict. First I had to deal with my own perceptions. The rest would follow.

So I came up with an exercise; I would repeat constantly, out loud when I could and silently when other people were present: "I forgive you Mike, and I release you to the Holy Spirit. I forgive you Mike, and I release you to the Holy Spirit. I forgive you Mike, and I release you to the Holy Spirit."

Since Mike didn't call the day after our early morning phone call or the day after, or the day after that, I had a lot of negative feelings to try to dissipate. My forgiveness chant—a kind of mantra, or repeated affirmation of spiritual wisdom—worked like a healing balm on my emotional turmoil. It deterred my temptation to focus on Mike's behavior, and kept me focused on my own feelings instead. My goal was inner peace, and I knew I couldn't have that as long as I perceived him as guilty.

In case you're wondering, it took him two weeks to call. The constant repetition of "I forgive you Mike, and I release you to the Holy Spirit," this willingness to forgive someone, had worked on my brain like a pleasurable drug. I didn't care whether I heard from him again or not.

So one day I'm in my house, the phone rings, and I hear Mike's familiar voice. "Marianne?"

Before I could even think about it consciously, a real warmth and love filled up my chest. "Mike? Hi! It's so good to hear from you!" And it was. It felt wonderful to hear his voice.

"How are you doing? I've missed you." (Can you *believe* he said that?!?)

I don't know if I said I'd missed him, too. His line was so ridiculous, I probably didn't say anything. But I do remember this: He said, "Well, when can I see you?"

I said, "When would you like to?"

"How about tonight?"

At that moment, words came out of my mouth that startled me as much as they must have startled him. I said with a lot of love and kindness, "Mike, I really care for you and that's not going to change. I'm still your friend no matter what. But when it comes to dating, we don't seem to do the same dance. So if you want to have lunch sometime, please call. But as far as a date is concerned, I need to pass."

We both mumbled a few more pleasantries and then got off the phone. I was worried that I had rejected a brother, but just as that worry came into my mind, I saw an internal image of lots of champagne bottles with their corks popping off in the middle of Heaven. I hadn't rejected a brother. I had simply accepted myself in a whole new way. He had a win—a lesson learned and a friendship if he wanted it—and I had a win. Forgiveness hadn't turned me into a doormat. It had taught me how to own my yes and own my no, without anger, with dignity and with love.

15.   COMMUNICATING LOVE

"To communicate is to join and to attack is to separate."

The Holy Spirit accepts people unconditionally. To the ego, this is an outrageous thought, because unconditional love is the death of the ego. How will people grow if we all go around just accepting each other as we are all the time? Accepting people as they are has the miraculous effect of helping them improve. Acceptance doesn't prohibit growth; rather, it fosters it.

People who are always telling us what's wrong with us don't help us so much as they paralyze us with shame and guilt. People who accept us help us to feel good about ourselves, to relax, to find our way. Accepting another person doesn't mean we never share constructive suggestions. But like everything else, our behavior is not so much the issue as the energy that it carries. If I'm criticizing someone in order to change them, that's my ego talking. If I've prayed and asked God to heal me of my judgment, however, and then I'm still led to communicate something, the style of my sharing will be one of love instead of fear. It won't carry the energy of attack, but rather of support. Behavioral change is not enough.

Covering an attack with sugary icing, with a sweet tone of voice or therapeutic jargon, is not a miracle. A miracle is an authentic switch from fear to love. When we speak from the ego, we will call up the ego in others. When we speak from the Holy Spirit, we will call up their love. A brother who is in error, says the Course, calls for teaching, not attack.

The following section in the Course is a powerful guide to right-minded communication in relationships.

> *"Errors are of the ego, and correction of errors lies in the relinquishment of the ego. When you correct a brother, you are telling him that he is wrong. He may be making no sense at the time, and it is certain that, if he is speaking from the ego, he will not be making sense. But your task is still to tell him he is right. You do not tell him this verbally, if he is speaking foolishly. He needs correction at another level, because his error is at another level. He is still right, because he is a Son of God."*

Miracles are created in an invisible realm. The Holy Spirit improves our style. He teaches us how to communicate from love instead of attack. Often people will say, "Well, I told *them*. I really communicated!" But communication is a two-way street. It only occurs if one person speaks, and the other one can hear them. We've all been in conversations where two people spoke and no one heard a thing. We've also had conversations where no one said anything and both people understood everything perfectly. In order to truly communicate, we must take responsibility for the heart space that exists between us and another. It is that heart space, or the absence of it, which will determine whether communication is miraculous or fearful. Sometimes, of course, that means keeping our mouths shut. Silence can be a powerfully loving communication. There have been times when I was wrong, and I knew I was wrong, and I knew they knew I was wrong, and I loved them for having the graciousness not to say anything. It gave me a chance to recoup with dignity.

When we do speak, the key to communication is not what we say, but rather the attitude that lies behind what we say. Since there is only one mind, all of us are telepathically communicating all the time. Every moment, we are choosing to join or to separate, and the person to whom we're speaking feels what we have chosen regardless of our words. The choice to join is the key to communication because it is the key to communion. The point is not to seek our goal in a communication, but to find a pure ground of being from which to mount our message. We don't seek joining through our words; we accept the thought that we are joined with the other person before we speak. That acceptance is itself a miracle.

The teacher of God is a finely-tuned intuitional instrument. *A Course in Miracles* says we're to listen to our brother, first and foremost. If we're supposed to speak, He'll let us know. Jesus once sent His disciples out into the countryside and told them to teach the gospel. "What shall we say?" they asked Him. His answer was, "I'll tell you when you get there." We're not to try to figure out what to say to a brother. It is merely our job to ask the Holy Spirit to purify our perceptions of the other person. From that place within, and only from that place, will we find the power of words and the power of silence, which bring the peace of God.

16.   COMMITMENT

"Whom God hath brought together, the ego cannot put asunder."

A Course in Miracles says we are to have total commitment in all of our relationships, and they will never compete with one another. Commitment in a relationship means commitment to the process of mutual understanding and forgiveness—no matter how many conversations it takes, nor how uncomfortable those conversations might sometimes be.

When we physically separate from someone we've been involved with, that doesn't mean the relationship is over. Relationships are eternal. The "separation" is another chapter in the relationship. Often, letting go of the old form of the relationship becomes a lesson in pure love much deeper than any that would have been learned had the couple stayed together. At the so-called end of relationships, I have sometimes felt like I was falling in love with the person more deeply than I had been before. What I've discovered for myself is that the Holy Spirit sometimes pulls out all the stops at that moment, simply because it takes all the love we're capable of to let a person go. "I love you so much that I can release you to be where you need to be, to go where you need to go." This moment in a relationship is not about an ending. It's about the ultimate fulfillment of the purpose in any relationship: that we find the meaning of pure love.

Sometimes the lesson to be learned in a relationship is how to hang in there and try to work things out. Other times, the lesson to be learned is how to exit a situation that doesn't serve. No one can determine for another person what principle applies in what circumstance. It is ultimately our connection to the Holy Spirit, our own intuitional guidance, that alone can lead us to the higher unfoldment of events through the deepest understanding.

I have said in many lectures, "Never abandon a person when you're leaving." What does that mean? It means that it's important for us to honor the eternal nature of relationships. When relationships change form, their content need not be diminished. The ego says, "Look, it's over with them. It didn't work out. We're no longer together. What was, was. I'm with someone new now." The "ex" becomes a second-rate citizen. Often the new mate feels justified in saying, "Why are you talking to *them*? *We're* together now." Woe to the person who doesn't support the healing between a man or woman and their ex. Ultimately you discover that how the person treated the last one is exactly how they'll treat you. We feel jealousy, the need to hold on to what we've got, because in this area, as in every other, the ego says that there's only so much love to go around, that another person's good takes away from our own. The ego is a belief in finite resources, but love is infinite. Whenever love is added to any part of the system, there is an increase to every part. Love only gives rise to more love. If my husband or boyfriend heals with his past relationships, it only increases his capacity to love me from a healed and whole place. The last woman in his life is not my competition. She is my sister.

A man I once knew came over to my house for dinner. We had been dating a short time, and I asked him what he had been doing all day. He told me he had been working on a script with his last girlfriend, who was still his writing partner. He told me that they had gotten into a pretty sticky conversation about their relationship. She was still hurt, having a hard time letting go, the same stuff we all know. I asked him how they had left it. He said she was pretty upset. I put down the food I was preparing, looked him in the eye and said, "Go call her." The thought of that woman being on the other side of town somewhere, enduring that horrible anxiety while we sat down to a romantic dinner, was hard for me to bear. I had been in her place. How totally unethical it would have been for me not to support that woman in her feelings.

"You don't mind?" he said.

"Not at all," I told him. "Dinner can wait."

Our needs are not separate. If we contribute to another person's pain, it will always come back to haunt us. If we do what we can to help them, someone will always come around to do the same for us. It's not enough to sit idly by while others hurt, using the catch-all phrase "It's not my responsibility" or "It would be codependent of me to get involved" as an excuse for a selfish stance. A woman once said to me after a situation in which I felt betrayed, "I never intended to hurt you." I said, "But you never intended to love me, either." Love is not neutral. It takes a stand. It is a commitment to the attainment of the conditions of peace for everyone involved in a situation.

17.   FAITH IN RELATIONSHIPS

"Faith is the acknowledgement of union."

Often we long for another person because, in an invisible, intangible realm, we're still communicating, still connecting, still seeking resolution. People will say, "You're being neurotic. It's time to let go." But there was a time when widows wore weeds for a year; grief was understood, acknowledged, validated. It's not neurotic to grieve a relationship; what's neurotic is when we don't. On some level, no matter how disassociated from our feelings we might be, every relationship brings hope—hope that this might be a safe place, a haven, a rest after all our battles.

When a relationship doesn't work out, for whatever reason, our disappointment is natural. Every intense encounter represents a deep and complicated karmic connection. An ending relationship is much like a death, and in many cases the sadness is even greater. When someone has died, there has often been completion and understanding that doesn't occur when both people are alive but have separated without higher awareness. Perhaps the one we love is simply on the other side of town now, sleeping with someone else, yet they are really universes away since the resolution we so crave has not occurred. There's no need to pretend this isn't a knife to the heart. It is, and there's nothing to do but cry the tears that gush forth like blood from a wound.

Now is the time for faith. Let us be softened by our tears. When emotional knives hit the heart, walls crumble that didn't belong there to begin with. We can learn then. We can learn what is illusion and what is real. We can learn that idols can never ever be trusted, and we can learn about a love that never, ever leaves.

There are many conflicts in relationships that try our faith. One of them is betrayal. Betrayal is a word that we don't really understand until it's happened to us. There's an unparalleled pain when a friend is the one who's holding the knife.

In the Course, Jesus says that although, according

to the thinking of the world, he was betrayed, he didn't choose that perception for himself. In other words, he knew that he couldn't really be betrayed, because what isn't love isn't real. So when we are attacked, when the medicine is so bitter that it takes all our power not to crumble as we take it, what do we do then? Where is our solace?

Someone once told me that the way peacock feathers are made is from peacocks eating thorns. What a beautiful image, that the harsh things we have to digest can contribute to our beauty. But not always. Only when we open up enough to really take in the horror, oddly enough. Resistance and defense only make the error more real, and increase our pain.

If Jesus had yelled from the cross, "I hate all you guys," it would have been a completely different story. There would have been no resurrection. What created the space for his triumph was his defenselessness, his holding to love despite what others were doing to him. The body can be destroyed, but truth cannot be. Truth will always reassert itself, given a symbolic three days. Three days represents the time it takes between the crucifixion and the resurrection, between an open-hearted response to hurt and the experience of rebirth that will always follow.

How often I've said to myself and others, "This is just the three days. Hold on. Hold on." When our friends have turned against us, or we have been cheated or lied about, the temptation is so strong to defend, attack back. But the Course says that "in our defenselessness, our safety lies." It is one more place where our power comes from saying, "I will step back and let Him lead the way." The Christ within us can handle any assault because it is not affected by lovelessness. Only our belief that we are affected by fear can make it affect us. Defense is a way of agreeing with the attacker in the power of his attack, and so making it real in our experience.

It takes great courage and personal strength to hold on to our center during times of great hurt. It takes wisdom to understand that our reactiveness only fans the flames of false drama. Love creates a mystical shield around us, protecting us from chaos. When we are in the midst of loss, or betrayal, or crisis of any kind, there is power in the words, "Be still and know I am." Truth can never be destroyed. There is no loss except in time, says the Course, and time does not exist.

18.   MARRIAGE

"You undertook, together, to invite the Holy Spirit into your relationship."

Marriage, like everything else, can be used by either the ego or the Holy Spirit. Its content is never predetermined. It is a living organism that reflects the continuous choices of the individuals involved.

Very little is sacred anymore in this world, but one

thing must be treated with reverence or else the moral fabric of the world disintegrates: an agreement between two people. An enlightened marriage is a commitment to participate in the process of mutual growth and forgiveness, sharing a common goal of service to God.

A man once told me that his relationship with his ex-wife worked beautifully for the first year they were together. At that time they were both actively involved in an organization dedicated to personal growth. Once they left the organization, however, the marriage fell apart. This doesn't indicate that the marriage had nothing going for it anyway. Rather, it reveals the importance of a context bigger than the personal concerns of one or even both parties.

Why is marriage a more profound commitment than other forms of relationship, such as a couple who are living together? Because it is an agreement that, while a whole lot of shaking and screaming might go on, no one's going to leave the room. We are both safe to go through whatever emotion is called forth from deep within us— and whenever we are truthful, there are times when we are upset—but it is safe to do that here. No one is leaving.

The commitment of marriage is publicly declared. When guests are present at a wedding and the ceremony is a religious one, a ritual is performed in which collective prayers form a circle of light and protection around the relationship.

A marriage is God's gift to a man and woman. It is a gift that should then be given back to Him. A man's wife is literally God's gift to Him. A woman's husband is God's gift to her. But God only gives gifts that are meant for everyone. So it is that a marriage is meant to be a blessing on the world, because it is a context in which two people might become more than they would have been alone. The entire world is blessed by the presence of healed people. One of the Course's Workbook exercises reads, "When I am healed, I am not healed alone."

A partner's support and forgiveness enable us to stand forth more magnificently in the world. *A Course in Miracles* tells us that love is not meant to be exclusive, but inclusive. Several years ago there was a popular song that included the refrain, "You and me against the world." If any man ever said that to me, I'd tell him I was switching sides. We don't get married to escape the world; we get married to heal it together.

Under the Holy Spirit's guidance, a married couple commit to the creation of a context in which their individual resources—material, emotional and spiritual—are placed in each other's service. As we give, so shall we receive. Service does not mean self-sacrifice. It means giving the needs of another person the same priority as our own. The ego claims that one person wins at the expense of another. The Holy Spirit enters into any situation bringing a win for everyone involved. In marriage we have a wonderful opportunity to see through the illusion of separate needs. The married couple is not to think only in terms of what's good for him or her, but rather what is good for them. This is one of the many ways in which marriage can be part of the healing of the Son of God.

As with anything else, the key to a successful marriage is the conscious awareness of God. The marriage is surrendered to Him to be used for His purposes. The saying that the family that prays together stays together, is true. The enlightened marriage includes the presence of a mystical third. The Holy Spirit is asked to guide perceptions, thoughts, feelings and actions in order that in this, as in all things, God's will might be done on earth as it is in Heaven.

19.   FORGIVING OUR PARENTS, OUR FRIENDS, OURSELVES

"The holiest of all spots on earth is where an ancient hatred has become a present love."

There is no coming to consciousness without forgiving our parents. Whether we like it or not, our mother is our primary image of an adult woman, and our father is our primary image of an adult man. If we hold grievances against our mother, then if we are a man, we will not be able to escape the projection of guilt onto other adult women who come into our lives; and if we are a woman, we will not be able to escape self-condemnation as we grow into our womanhood. If we hold grievances against our father, then if we are a woman, we will not be able to escape projection of guilt onto other adult men who come into our lives; and if we are a man, we will not be able to escape self-condemnation as we grow into our manhood.

That's it. At a certain point, we forgive because we *decide* to forgive. Healing occurs in the present, not the past. We are not held back by the love we didn't receive in the past, but by the love we're not extending in the present. Either God has the power to renew our lives, or He doesn't. Could God be looking at any of us and saying, "I'd love to give you a joyful life, but your mother was so terrible, my hands are tied"?

There is a lot of talk today about people growing up in dysfunctional homes. Who *didn't* grow up in a dysfunctional home! This world is dysfunctional! But there is nothing we have been through, or seen, or done, that cannot be used to make our lives more valuable now. We can grow from any experience, and we can transcend any experience. This kind of talk is blasphemy to the ego, which respects pain, glorifies pain, worships pain, and creates pain. Pain is its centerpiece. It sees forgiveness as its enemy.

Forgiveness remains the only path that leads out of hell. Whether we're forgiving our parents, someone else, or ourselves, the laws of mind remain the same: As we love, we shall be released from pain, and as we deny love, we shall remain in pain. Every moment, we're either extending love or projecting fear, and every thought takes us nearer to Heaven or hell. What will it take to make us remember that the ark is entered two by two, that there is no getting into Heaven without taking someone with you?

Practice and commitment are the keys to love. What I've seen for myself, and witnessed others grapple with also, is not an argument with the power of love. I can see the truth of all these principles. But I have also seen how often I would resist the experience of love, when holding on to a grievance seems more important than letting it go. An entire world has been built on fear. Fear's system will not be dismantled in a moment. We can work on ourselves every moment that we live. The world is healed one loving thought at a time. Mother Theresa said that there are no great deeds—just small deeds done with great love.

Each of us have different fears, and different manifestations of fear, but all of us are saved by the same technique: the call to God to save our lives by salvaging our minds. "Lead us not into temptation, but deliver us from evil, for Love is the Kingdom, and Love is the glory, and Love is the power, forever and ever."

CHAPTER 7

Work

*"I am only here to be truly helpful.
I am here to represent Him who sent me.
I do not have to worry about what to say or what
to do, because He Who sent me will direct me.
I am content to be wherever He wishes, knowing
He goes there with me.
I will be healed as I let Him teach me to heal."*

1. SURRENDERING OUR CAREERS

"Seeing your strengths exactly as they are, and equally aware of where they can be best applied, for what, to whom and when, He chooses and accepts your part for you."

Success means we go to sleep at night knowing that our talents and abilities were used in a way that served others. We're compensated by grateful looks in people's eyes, whatever material abundance supports us in performing joyfully and at high energy, and the magnificent feeling that we did our bit today to save the world.

The Atonement means putting love first. In everything. In business as well as everything else. You're in business to spread love. Your screenplay should spread love. Your hair salon should spread love. Your agency should spread love. Your life should spread love. The key to a successful career is realizing that it's not separate from the rest of your life, but is rather an extension of your most basic self. And your most basic self is love.

Knowing who you are and why you came here—that you are a child of God and that you came here to heal and be healed—is more important than knowing what you want to do. What you want to do is not the important question. The question to ask is, "When I do *anything*, how should I do it?" And the answer is, "Kindly." People don't normally associate business with kindness, because business has come to be regarded as simply a tool for making money. Miracle-workers are not in business only to make money; they're in business to inject love into the world.

Each of us has a particular part to play in "God's plan for salvation." The Holy Spirit's job is to reveal to us our function and to help us perform it. The Holy Spirit asks us if it's reasonable to assume that He would assign us a task, and then not provide us with the means of its accomplishment.

Once again, we're not deciding for ourselves what part to play in life, but rather asking that it be revealed to us where He would have us go and what He would have us do. We surrender our careers to Him. During World War II, the Allied generals oversaw all troop activity from a central headquarters, from which they issued orders. The commanders on various fronts didn't necessarily know how their movements fit into an overall military scheme: they just knew they did, because they knew there was a general intelligence behind the issuing of their orders. So it is with us. We might not know how or where our talents would best be put to use, but the Holy Spirit does. *A Course in Miracles* teaches us to avoid self-initiated plans, and to instead surrender our plans to God.

Some people have said, "But I'm afraid to surrender my career to God. I'm a musician—what if He wants me to be an accountant?" My answer to that is, why would He? Wouldn't He rather have someone who understands numbers do that job?

If you're talented at music, that talent is of God. If something makes your heart sing, that's God's way of telling you it's a contribution He wants you to make. Sharing our gifts is what makes us happy. We're most powerful, and God's power is most apparent on the earth when we're happy.

A Course in Miracles says that the only real pleasure comes from doing God's will. The crux of salvation in any area is a shift in our sense of purpose. Relationships, careers, bodies—all these areas of our lives are reborn in spirit when we dedicate them to God's purposes, asking that they be used as instruments through which the world is healed.

That shift is a miracle. As always, we consciously ask for it. "Dear God, please give my life some sense of purpose. Use me as an instrument of your peace. Use my talents and abilities to spread love. I surrender my job to you. Help me to remember that my real job is to love the world back to health. Thank you very much. Amen."

2.   GOD'S WILL

> *"Where would you have me go?*
> *What would you have me do?*
> *What would you have me say, and to whom?"*

People ask themselves, "Do I want to serve God, or do I want to be happy?" Since certain organized religions have represented the spiritual life as a life of sacrifice and austerity, it can be hard for some people to imagine that a life lived close to God is a life full of joy. *A Course in Miracles* says the only real pleasure comes from doing God's will.

God does not demand sacrifice. The life of sacrifice is the life we live *before* we find a higher sense of identity and purpose: the sacrifice of the memory of how magnificent we really are, and what an important job we came here to do. And that's a lot to sacrifice, because when we can't remember why we're going somewhere, we have a hard time acting on full throttle once we get there. Love gives energy and direction. It's spiritual fuel.

Any career, when given to the Holy Spirit, can be used as part of the plan of the restoration of the world. No job is too big or too small for God to use. You have the unlimited power of the universe within you and so does everyone else. It's nothing to take personal credit for, nor anything to feel guilty about. Our real power emanates from a force that's in us but not of us. Be humble before God, says the Course, yet great in him. Remembering this keeps us connected to our innocence, and as long as we have that, the power will keep pouring through us. Forget it, and the faucet could be turned off at any moment. Stop blessing the universe, and the universe will seem to stop blessing you. Whatever your activity, just ask that it be used to bless the world.

I remember one day complaining to my girlfriend June how unhappy I was, and she said, "Marianne, I don't mean to be hard on you, but do you ever do anything for anyone else?" That comment felt like a brick to my forehead, although I did very little about it at the time. After I went through my period of very deep depression several years later, however, human suffering became a much more personally significant subject. I thought that if other people suffered a fraction as much as I had, then my heart burst for them and I wanted to be of help. God seemed to say to me then, "People suffer deeply, and there have been people suffering around you all your life. You just didn't notice. You were shopping."

I used to worry, as do many people, about what I was supposed to do with my life. I never seemed to be able to stick with any one thing very long or make money or find any real satisfaction in my work. I felt paralyzed. I remember once asking God to reveal to me what He wanted me to know in order that I might change. I got down on my knees and worked myself into a grandiose meditative state. I saw visual images of a glorious sky and a group of angels marching through the clouds to bring me His answer. A couple of cherubs held up a scroll that they then began to unfold. My heart started racing as I awaited God's message, which I was sure would be extremely important. Slowly the letters on the scroll began to form words: "Marianne, you're a spoiled brat."

The reason I was paralyzed was because I had lost touch with the sole memory of why I came to earth. Telling me I was a spoiled brat was the perfect information, the key to unlock my energies. The problem was my selfishness. Like actors who have spent so much time learning how to act that they didn't learn how to live, and so end up making lousy actors because they ultimately have nothing authentic to reveal about life, we sometimes lose our personal power by forgetting why we have it. We study up on how to run businesses, not stopping to think about *why* we're in business except to make money. This is not a spiritually powerful beam, and the universe will tolerate it less and less as the nineties unfold.

3.   PERSONAL POWER

"All power is of God."

Don't ask God to send you a brilliant career, but rather ask Him to show you the brilliance within you. It is the recognition of our brilliance that releases it into expression. Stable, meaningful external effects don't occur until we've experienced an internal stirring. Once an internal stirring has occurred, external effects cannot fail to happen. We're all capable of an internal stirring, and are in fact coded for it. It is our potential for greatness. Achievement doesn't come from what we do, but from who we are. Our worldly power results from our personal power. Our career is an extension of our personality.

People who profoundly achieve aren't necessarily people who do so much; they're people around whom things get done. Mahatma Gandhi and President Kennedy were both examples of this. Their greatest achievements lay in all the energy they stirred in other people, the invisible forces they unleashed around them. By touching their own depths, they touched the depths within others.

That kind of charisma, the power to effect what happens on the earth from an invisible realm within, is the natural right and function of the Son of God. The word "charisma" was originally a religious term. It means "of the spirit." The new frontiers are internal ones. The real stretch is always within us. Instead of expanding our ability or willingness to go out and get anything, we expand our ability to receive what is already here for us.

Personal power emanates from someone who takes life seriously. The universe takes us as seriously as we take it. There is no greater seriousness than the full appreciation of the power and importance of love. Miracles flow from the recognition that love is the purpose of our careers.

A Course in Miracles discusses a traditional Christian concept called "the gifts of the Holy Spirit." This idea is that, when our lives are given to the Holy Spirit to use for His purposes, new talents emerge within us. We don't get our lives together and then give them to God, but rather we give our lives to God and then things start coming together. As our hearts open, our talents and gifts begin to blossom. Many people have told me that once they're successful and have made a lot of money, they will use that success to help the world. But that's a delay technique by which the ego tries to keep us from showing up fully in our own lives. Even if we don't yet consider ourselves successful, we can devote our work now to being used in the service of the healing of the world. From that point of power our careers will take off.

No matter what we do, we can make it our ministry. No matter what form our job or activity takes, the content is the same as everyone else's: we are here to minister to human hearts. If we talk to anyone, or see anyone, or even think of anyone, then we have the opportunity to bring more love into the universe. From a waitress to the head of a movie studio, from an elevator operator to the president of a nation, there is no one whose job is unimportant to God.

When you know this, when you fully live up to the opportunity to heal, you achieve an energy that pushes you forward in worldly endeavors. Love makes you more attractive. That means you attract, like a magnet. You don't just attract people; you attract various circumstances that reflect back to you the power of your devotion. Your personal power is not something that is going to reveal itself at some later date. Your power is a result of your decision to reveal it. You are powerful in whatever moment you choose to be. The choice to be used as an instrument of love, right here, right now, is a choice for personal empowerment.

A Course in Miracles tells us that all of the children of God have power—yet no one has "special" power. All of us are special, and yet none of us are special. No one has any more potential than anyone else for spreading the love and light of God. Many of our traditional notions of success rely on our talking ourselves into the belief that we're special and we have something special to offer. The truth is, none of us are special because special people would be different and separate from others. The oneness of Christ makes this impossible. The belief in specialness, therefore, is delusional and thus breeds fear.

What a Beethoven, Shakespeare or Picasso has done is not *create* something, so much as they have accessed that place within themselves from which they could *express* that which has been created by God. Their genius then, is actually expression and not creation. That's why great art strikes us with the shock of recognition, the wish that *we* had said that. The soul thrills at the reminder of what we all already know.

The Course says that one day, all the gifts of God will be shared equally by everyone. We all have the potential for greatness, but it gets plowed out of us early. Fear entered when someone told us there's a first prize, second prize and third prize, that some efforts deserve an A, and some get a C. After a while, part of us becomes afraid to even try. The only thing we have to give to the world is our own grasp on it. The ego argues that this is not enough. It leads us to cover up our simple truth, to try to invent a better one. But the ego isn't protecting us here, although, as always, it pretends to. It isn't guarding against our making fools of ourselves; it is guarding against our experience of who we really are, the brilliance of expressing it, and the joy that the expression brings to ourselves and others.

I love the story of the little girl who showed her teacher a picture she painted of a tree. The tree was purple. The teacher said, "Sweetheart, I've never seen a purple tree, now have I?"

"Oh?" said the little girl. "That's too bad."

We can't fake authenticity. We think we need to create ourselves, always doing a paste-up job on our personalities. That is because we're trying to be special rather than real. We're pathetically trying to conform with all the other people trying to do the same.

A tulip doesn't strive to impress anyone. It doesn't struggle to be different than a rose. It doesn't have to. It *is* different. And there's room in the garden for every flower. You didn't have to struggle to make your face different than anyone else's on earth. It just is. You *are* unique because you were created that way. Look at little children in kindergarten. They're all different without trying to be. As long as they're unselfconsciously being themselves, they can't help but shine. It's only later, when children are taught to compete, to strive to be better than others, that their natural light becomes distorted.

The natural light of God within us all is what the Course refers to as our grandeur. The ego's efforts to embellish our natural state is what the Course refers to as grandiosity. "It is easy to distinguish grandeur from grandiosity," says the Course, "because love is returned and pride is not." The ego interferes with the clear expression of our power by trying to get us to add something to it. This is actually a ploy by which it thwarts our capacity to express who we really are, and accept full recognition from others in return.

Once again, separation is the ego's goal. I used to always be on an emotional roller-coaster ride, feeling I was better than other people, and then feeling I was worse. "I'm better, no I'm not as good, I'm better, no I'm not as good." They're the same mistake. The truth is, we're just like everybody else. Knowing this—that we're no better or worse than anyone else because we're all essentially the same—is a thought lacking in luster only until we fully appreciate what kind of club we belong to. Humanity is a group of infinitely powerful creatures. Our power, however, is in us but not of us. It is God's spirit inside of us that enlightens and enlivens our lives. Of ourselves we're really no big deal.

This thought has helped me in my career. I walk onto a stage and sometimes speak to more than a thousand people at a time. I can't imagine dealing with the pressure of having to convince myself that I have something special to offer. I don't try to. I don't have to impress anyone, and if I'm not thinking that I have to, there's nothing to do but relax. I walk out on stage without feeling the need to make people think I'm special, because I know I'm not. I just talk to friends, casually and with enthusiasm. That's it. There isn't anything else. Everything else is just an illusion. The Son of God doesn't have to embellish who he is.

We're tempted to think that we're more impressive when we put on airs. We're not, of course; we're rather pathetic when we do that. The Course states, "Grandiosity is always a cover for despair." The light of Christ shines most brightly within us when we relax and let it be, allowing it to shine away our grandiose delusions. But we're afraid to let down our masks. What is really happening here, unconsciously, is not that we are defending against our smallness. The ego is actually, in those moments, defending against God.

Our deepest fear is not that we are inadequate. Our deepest fear is that we are powerful beyond measure. It is our light, not our darkness, that most frightens us. We ask ourselves, Who am I to be brilliant, gorgeous, talented, fabulous? Actually, who are you *not* to be? You are a child of God. Your playing small doesn't serve the world. There's nothing enlightened about shrinking so that other people won't feel insecure around you. We are all meant to shine, as children do. We were born to make manifest the glory of God that is within us. It's not just in some of us; it's in everyone. And as we let our own light shine, we unconsciously give other people permission to do the same. As we're liberated from our own fear, our presence automatically liberates others.

A miracle worker is an artist of the soul. There's no higher art than living a good life. An artist informs the world of what's available behind the masks we all wear. That's what we're all here to do. The reason so many of us are obsessed with becoming stars is because we're not yet starring in our own lives. The cosmic spotlight isn't pointed *at* you; it radiates from *within* you. I used to feel like I was waiting for someone to discover me, to "produce" me, like Lana Turner at the drugstore. Ultimately I realized that the person I was waiting for was myself. If we wait for the world's permission to shine, we will never receive it. The ego doesn't give that permission. Only God does, and He has already done so. He has sent you here as His personal representative and is asking you to channel His love into the world. Are you waiting for a more important job? There isn't one.

There is a plan for each of us, and each of us is precious. As we open our hearts more and more, we're moved in the directions in which we're supposed to go. Our gifts well up inside of us and extend of their own accord. We accomplish effortlessly.

How could Leonardo da Vinci not have painted? How could Shakespeare not have written? In *Letters to a Young Poet*, Rilke tells a young writer to write only if he *has* to. We are to do what there is a deep psychological and emotional imperative for us to do. That's our point of power, the source of our brilliance. Our power is not rationally or willfully called forth. It's a divine dispensation, an act of grace.

4.   MONEY

"Joy has no cost."

Do what you love. Do what makes your heart sing. And *never do it for the money.* Don't go to work to make money; go to work to spread joy. Seek ye first the kingdom of Heaven, and the Maserati will get here when it's supposed to.

God doesn't have a poverty consciousness. He doesn't want you to have a boring life or a boring career. He doesn't have anything against the things of this world. Money isn't evil; it's just nothing. Like anything else, it can be used for holy or unholy purposes.

I once had a small bookstore. A man came in one day and told me that he was going to teach me how to make money. "Every person that walks in that door," he said, "is a potential sale. And that's what you should silently say to yourself whenever a customer walks into the store: Potential sale, potential sale."

His advice sounded exploitative to me. He was advising me to view other people as pawns in my own scheme. I prayed and received these words: "Your store is a church." Church, esoterically, means the gathering of souls. It's not an outer plane but rather an inner plane phenomenon. People don't come into your place of business so that you can *get* anything. They're sent so that you can give them love.

After I said the prayer and got the feeling that my store was a church, I understood that my only job was to love the people who came there. I actually did that: every time I saw a customer walk in, I would silently bless them in some way or another. Not everyone bought a book every time they came in, but people began to consider me their bookseller. Customers were attracted to a peaceful feeling in the air. People might not know where it comes from, but they can feel it when love is being sent in their direction.

I'm amazed when I walk into stores and the sales people are rude, as if they're doing you some kind of favor letting you be there. A rude attitude is destructive to the emotional fabric of the world. Where I grew up, we left a store with that kind of energy because it doesn't feel good to be there.

When our goal is making money, creativity becomes distorted. If I saw money as the ultimate goal of my teaching career, then I would have to think more about what people wanted to hear and less about what I feel it's important to say. My energy would become tainted with efforts to get people to come back, to sell them on my lectures, to get them to bring their friends. But if the purpose of my career is to channel God's love, then I'm only there to open my heart, open my brain and open my mouth.

When we're working solely for money, our motivation is getting rather than giving. The miraculous transformation here is a shift from a sales mentality to a service mentality. Until we make this switch, we're operating from ego and concentrating on the things of this world rather than on love. This idolatry casts us into alien emotional territory, where we are always afraid. We're afraid of either failure or success. If we're closer to success, we'll fear success. If we're closer to failure, we'll fear failure. The issue isn't success or failure. The issue is the presence of fear, and its inevitability wherever love is absent.

Like everything else, money is either holy or unholy, depending on the purposes ascribed to it by the mind. We tend to do with money what we do with sex: we desire it but we judge the desire. It is the judgment that then distorts the desire, turning it into an ugly expression. Because we are ashamed to admit that we want these things, we have insidious ways of pretending that we don't—such as condemning our desires even as we act them out. The loss of purity is in us, then—not in money or in sex. They are both just canvasses onto which we project our guilt.

Just as the fearful mind is the source of promiscuity and sex is merely the vehicle through which it is expressed, so money is not the source of greed. The mind is the source of greed, and money is one of the places where it expresses itself. Both money and sex can be used for holy as well as unholy purposes. Like nuclear energy, the problem isn't the energy, but how it is applied.

Our judgment of wealth is actually an ego ploy to make sure we never have any. I was once driving around a very wealthy neighborhood in Houston and I thought, "These people work for huge multinational corporations that oppress people throughout the Third World." Then I stopped myself: How do *I* know what all those people do for a living, and how do I know what they do with their money? My judgmental attitude, masquerading as political consciousness, was actually my ego's way of trying to make sure that *I* would never have any money. What we mentally refuse to permit others, we refuse ourselves. What we bless in others, we draw to us.

When I was younger, I cherished the belief that, by being poor, I was somehow showing my camaraderie with the impoverished. Behind that thought, I see now, was my fear that I would fail if I tried to make money. I ultimately realized that poor people didn't need my sympathy so much as they needed cash. There's nothing pure or spiritual about poverty. We often see impoverished people who are very holy, but it isn't the poverty that creates the holiness. I've known some extremely spiritual wealthy people, and I've known some poor people who were anything but.

The Bible says it's harder for a rich man to get into Heaven than it is for a camel to walk through the eye of a needle. That's because the *attachment* to money is a huge temptation to deviate from love. But the moral imperative is not to block the reception of money into our lives. The challenge is to spiritualize our relationship to it, by seeing that its only purpose is to heal the world. In an enlightened society, rich people will not necessarily have less money. Poor people, however, will have much more. The problem, contrary to the ego's perception, is not just the distribution of wealth, but the consciousness around it. Money is not scarce. It is not a finite resource. We are not poor because the rich are rich. We are poor because we do not work with love.

It behooves us to remember that our money is God's money, and we want to have whatever He wants us to have in order to do with it whatever He wants us to do. God wants us to have whatever material support contributes to our greatest happiness. The ego tries to convince us that God demands sacrifice, and that the life of service would be a life of poverty. This is not the case. Our purpose on this earth is to be happy, and it is the Holy Spirit's function to help us achieve that. He leads us to whatever material abundance supports us in standing forth joyously within the world, without binding us further to it.

There's much work to be done for the healing of the world, and some of it costs money. Often the Holy Spirit sends us money so that we can perform tasks He wants accomplished on His behalf. A responsible attitude towards money is one in which we're open to whatever comes, and trusting that it always will.

In asking for miracles, we ask the Holy Spirit to remove the obstacles to our reception of money. These obstacles take the form of thoughts, such as: money is impure, or having money means we're greedy; rich people are bad, or I shouldn't make more money than my parents did. Having money means that we have more money with which to employ other people and heal the world. There's nothing beautiful about what happens to a society when money stops circulating.

One of the principles to remember about money is how important it is to pay for services rendered. If we begrudge someone else the right to make a living, we are begrudging ourselves the same. What we give, we will receive, and what we withhold will be withheld from us. And the universe doesn't register the difference between stealing from a huge corporation, or stealing from a nice little old lady.

The universe will always support our integrity. Sometimes our debts are so big or confusing, that even though we have the best of intentions, the burden and the guilt may be so overwhelming, that we just go on automatic, push the bills to the back of the drawer and try to forget them. Or change our phone number. The universe will not support that. A big person is not someone who never falls down. A big person is someone who, when they fall, does what it takes to get up again. As always, the issue is to ask for a miracle. There's no debtor's prison in this country. Once again, according to the Course, "Miracles are everyone's right but purification is necessary first."

Purity of heart creates breakthroughs. If you owe back bills, no matter how much, write a letter to the company or individual, own the issue, apologize if appropriate, and let them know that you are setting up a payment plan, effective immediately. Send them something with the letter. Don't set yourself up for failure. If you can't afford to send fifteen dollars a month, that's okay. Send five dollars, if that's all you can. But make sure you send it and send it regularly and on time. It doesn't matter if the bill is fifty thousand dollars. The Course says "there is no order of difficulty in miracles." No matter what the shape of a problem, its form or its size, a miracle can handle it. Miracles mean that at any moment we can begin again. No matter what the problem, as long as we return our minds to a graceful position now, the universe will always help us clean up the mess and start over. To repent means to think again. In every area, the universe will support us to the extent that we support it.

Most of us have a lot "on" money—anything from an inappropriate need for it to an inappropriate judgment of it. Many of us received strong messages about money during our childhoods. We were taught, verbally or nonverbally, that it is overly important, or unspiritual, or hard to get, or the root of all evil. Many of us are afraid that people won't like us if we don't make money, or afraid that they won't like us if we do. Money is an area where we need, individually and collectively, a radical healing of our mental habits.

We pray. "Dear God, I surrender to you all my thoughts about money, I surrender to you my debts, I surrender to you my wealth. Open my mind to receive abundantly. Channel your abundance through me in a way that serves the world. Amen."

5. *MINISTRY*

> *"And that one Voice appoints your function and relays it to you, giving you the strength to understand it, do what it entails, and to succeed in everything you do that is related to it."*

There's no more potent way to thank God for your gifts, or to increase them, than by sharing them. You will be given as much power in the world as you are willing to use on His behalf.

Think of your career as your ministry. Make your work an expression of love, in service to mankind. Within the worldly illusion, we all have different jobs. Some of us are artists, some of us are business people, some of us are scientists. But in the real world that lies beyond all this, we all have the same job: to minister to human hearts. All of us are here as ministers of God.

A few years ago I went back to Houston for a special reunion of my high school drama department. Our teacher was retiring, and ex-students of his from all over the country came to pay their respects. At the dinner, a lot of attention was given to the fact that many of Mr. Pickett's students had gone on to become successful actors. But many of his students had gone on to become successful people, period. By teaching us the truth about acting, he taught us the truth about life. Once you know: 1. Leave your personal problems at the stage door; 2. Treat the material with honesty, dignity and without embellishment; 3. Show up fully no matter how many people are in the audience, then you know everything you need to know in order to have a powerful professional career. To know the real truth about anything is to know the truth about everything. In learning the principles of ministry, we learn the principles of success, regardless of what form our ministry takes.

One of the things I've realized is that I've really only had one career. I've had many jobs, but they all had one basic element in common: me. The form of my work had mainly to do with where I was at that time in my life, and every form taught me something essential to my "career development."

As ministers of God, we let our careers be an expression of our own depth, of what really *matters* to us. Knowing that we are acting on behalf of a higher purpose than our own self-aggrandizement gives us the joy we're all seeking. Whatever we do, whatever our job, it can be a vessel through which we teach the message of salvation: that the Son of God is innocent, and we are all Sons of God. Kindness to Him transforms the world. We don't necessarily teach this verbally, but rather nonverbally. The problem most people have is that they're more concerned with the mode of their expression than with what they're seeking to express. That's because they don't *know* what they want to express. This generation, this culture, is full of people who want desperately to write a story, but for all the wrong reasons. I meet people who want to be in the spotlight, but have no idea what they would say if it was pointed at them. This is a fraudulent posture. It means we want the record contract more than the satisfaction of making music. The highest prize we can receive for creative work is the joy of being creative. Creative effort spent for any other reason than the joy of being in that light-filled place, love, God, whatever we want to call it, is lacking in integrity. It diminishes us. It reduces inspiration to mere sales.

A few years ago I visited Kauai. My friend and I took a ride on a boat along the Napali coastline. The boat was one of a fleet owned by a man known as Captain Zodiac. "Zodiac" is the word for the incredible land formations that meet the sea there. This man loved the coastline so passionately that he took the word for his own name. One day someone said to him, "You know a lot about this coastline and its history. A lot of people would love to see what you see here, and know what you know. Why don't you take people out on your boat and give them a tour?"

Captain Zodiac's rides are a great service to tourists on Kauai. They spread joy. They lift the cultural vibration. And the boat rides became quite a business.

Captain Zodiac now has lots of boats, and he's very successful. His business formed around his love.

The issue is whether we're working for money, or working for love. What we need to investigate is which one is the more abundant attitude. As with Captain Zodiac, and contrary to the ego's arguments, love is actually good business.

Any job can become a ministry, as long as it is dedicated to love. Your career can be an empty canvas for God to write on. Whatever your talents or abilities, He can use them. Our ministry becomes a joyous experience for ourselves and others as we let a mysterious force direct us. We simply follow instructions. We are allowing God's spirit to move through us, using our gifts and resources however He sees fit, to do His work in the world. This is the key to a successful career.

Success is not unnatural; it is the most natural thing in the world because it is the natural result of man's cocreation with God. In *A Movable Feast*, Hemingway writes about writing. He describes the difference between his writing a story, and a story writing itself. When he finds himself writing the story, he knows it's time to stop for the day. Our life is meant to be a story that mysteriously writes itself, and our work is the creative fruit of our lives.

"God, please use me" is the most powerful affirmation we can say for an abundant career. It is the miracle worker's prayer. Everybody wants a great job. Accept that it's already been given to you. The fact that you're alive means a function has been assigned to you: open your heart to everyone and everything. That way you're a vessel of God. Don't worry about what to say or what to do. He'll let you know.

I used to think I was lazy. I was always tired. Actually, I was just blocked until I discovered the purpose of my life. When our energy is applied in the direction of co-creating with God, of a willingness to supply love where there was none before, new energy bursts forth from deep inside us.

The world never gives you permission to shine. Only love does that. I remember being a cocktail waitress and walking into work one night thinking, "Oh, I get it! They think this is a bar!" As *A Course in Miracles* student, I now saw it differently. "This isn't a bar, and I'm not a waitress. That's just an illusion. Every business is a front for a church, and I'm here to purify the thought forms, to minister to the children of God." We can take our own lives seriously, regardless of whether or not anyone else does. No job really has any more potential impact on the planet than any other. We're always impacting the world in which we live, through our presence, our energy, our interactions with others. The question is, what kind of impact are we having?

I once knew a woman who wanted to be an actress, but wasn't getting work. In the meantime, she was working as a personal assistant to a professional writer. He adored her work and wanted her to travel with him all around the country, doing book tours, setting up lectures and helping him in various ways. Although she told me that she found working with him very exhilarating, she didn't want to leave Los Angeles because she felt she needed to be available in case there were acting jobs here that she might audition for.

"Nothing would be better for your acting career," I told my friend, "than that you would start starring in your own life." The reason many people want to be actors is not because they are truly called to the art, but rather because they want so desperately to create something beautiful in their own lives. Show up! Be enthusiastic! Put some energy into the life you're living now! How will anyone ever be impressed by your starlike quality if you're waiting to cultivate that quality until you become a star?

How would a miracle worker decide whether to go on the trip or stay in Los Angeles? We make decisions by asking that the Holy Spirit decide for us. There are always so many factors in life that we can't know. We make no decisions by ourselves, but ask how we might be most helpful in carrying out His plan. The moral authority that this attitude gives us creates a starlike quality. It is our humility, our desire to be of service, that makes us stars. Not our arrogance.

An ego thought that tempts a lot of people is the insistence that "I don't do windows." There's an old Zen tradition of disciples spending years dusting the altars of their masters as part of their preparation and training. The apprentice learns from being in the presence of the master, from serving him, and in time will surpass him. As the I Ching says, the universe fills up the modest and cuts down the proud. In modesty, we allow things to blossom. We're not ashamed to admit we're still in process. The ego emphasizes the goal rather than the process by which we achieve it. This is actually the ego's way of sabotaging us. We become proud and hardened, and thereby less attractive. There is nothing likable about false pride. It doesn't help us get work, or to get more successful.

Our job is to tend to our own growth as people, our grace and integrity and humility. We need no other goal. The core of our being then grows into a substantial power, externally as well as internally. Our ministry becomes a direct line of creation, from God through us to all mankind.

6. *NEW HEARTS, NEW JOBS*

> *"Child of God, you were created to create the good, the beautiful and the holy. Do not forget this."*

The ego says, "Your value is based on your credentials. You need a Ph.D. or its equivalent before you can get a good job." But some of the best and brightest of our generation were educated more by life than by school. There's a mass of talent in our society who have been everywhere and done everything, but have few credentials to show for it. Our achievements have been mainly internal.

Our ministries—our new careers—will reflect these internal achievements. They will express a new integration of mind and heart. They will express the consciousness of people contributing their individual resources to a general healing tide. These careers will be created as individual reflections of our unique talents. We will not "find" these jobs; we will create them. There are no ads in the "Help Wanted" section of newspapers for world saviors or miracle-workers. New forms of employment are emerging in response to new energies.

Carl Jung advised people to look closely into whatever fairy tales or myths particularly attracted them as children. When I was a child, I was enchanted by a fairy tale called "The Girl in the Patchwork Dress." In this story, the crown prince of a kingdom is going around the country looking for a bride. In one town, a huge ball is being held so that the Prince can have a chance to meet all the young ladies who live there. One girl wanted very much to go to the ball but she didn't have enough money to buy the material she would need in order to make a beautiful ball gown. So she did what she could. She picked up scraps of material from other girls' worktables, and put together a patchwork dress.

On the night of the ball, she entered the party and grew embarrassed when she saw how beautiful all the other girls' dresses were. Feeling ashamed, she hid in a closet. The prince came to the party, danced with all the girls there, and at a certain point, he had had enough. He was bored and he was going home. But as he was leaving, he noticed a piece of cloth sticking out of a closet door. He ordered his guards to open the door, where they discovered the girl in the patchwork dress. The prince danced with her, found her more interesting than any of the other girls, and he married her.

When I thought of that story as an adult, I knew why it had meant so much to me as a child. It revealed a significant archetype in my own life. I would ultimately taste a little bit of just about everything life had to offer. This would never earn me a degree in anything, but it would earn me a kind of overview. That vision of things would become the basis for my career. A lot of people among us are like the girl in the patchwork dress. We have a little bit of this, and a little bit of that. But you can't get a Ph.D. in having been everywhere and done everything. Put it all together, and we don't have a degree, but we're interesting people with interesting stories to tell. The patchwork dress symbolizes the consciousness of a generalist, one who synthesizes, while the other beautiful gowns symbolize the consciousness of a specialist. Both the generalist and the specialist are important viewpoints in the functioning of a healthy society.

Ultimately, it is not our credentials but our commitment to a higher purpose that creates our effectiveness in the world. Our resumes are important only if we think they are. I was eating dinner one night with a girlfriend of mine who is an excellent writer and a published author. I mentioned to another friend at the table, a man in publishing, that I thought Barbara should write a monthly column in one of the major women's magazines, called "The Healing Perspective" or "News from the Heartland" or something like that. Every month she could write some interesting piece about how an emotional breakthrough from fear to love had a healing impact in some personal or societal condition. I felt the column would give people hope.

But our friend in publishing took a different perspective. "Barbara couldn't do that," he said. "No magazine would publish it. She's not a Ph.D. She's not an authority. They won't see her as an established voice."

I wanted to turn to Barbara and place an invisible shield of cotton over her ears. I didn't want her to listen to his words. I didn't want her to believe his limited thinking. I didn't want her to close her mind to miracles.

I remember years ago, drinking a cup of coffee late one night as I had done many times before. "How can you do that?" a friend asked. "Won't that keep you up all night?" As of that night, coffee kept me up all night. I had never before, ever, made the conscious connection between coffee and caffeine and sleeplessness, and so, in my experience, there had never been one. Neither need there be an automatic connection between a lack of credentials and a lack of opportunity.

The desire to serve God creates the means by which we do so. Our power doesn't lie in our resume or our connections. Our power doesn't lie in what we've done or even in what we're doing. Our power lies in our clarity about why we're on the earth. We'll be important players if we think that way. And the important players of the coming years will be the people who see themselves as here to contribute to the healing of the world. Everything else is trivial in comparison. Where you went to school is no big deal, or even whether you went to school at all. God can use the flimsiest resume. He can use the smallest gifts. Whatever our gift is to God, however humble it may seem, He can turn it into a mighty work on His behalf. Our greatest gift to Him is our devotion. From that point of power, doors open. Careers blossom. We heal, and the world around us heals.

7.   GOALS

"God is the only goal I have today."

Goal-setting has become very popular in recent years. It is a process of focusing the mind on a desired result. This is actually just another way of trying to get the world to do what we want it to do. It is not spiritual surrender.

A Course in Miracles discusses a difference between "magic and miracles." Magic is when we focus the mind on a desired manifestation, giving our shopping list to God and telling Him what we want Him to do for us. Miracles are when we ask God what we can do for Him.

Miracles shift us from a "get" to a "give" mentality. The desire to get something reflects a core belief that we don't have enough already. As long as we believe there is scarcity inside us, we'll continue to manufacture scarcity around us because that is our basic thought. No matter what we get, it will never be enough.

When our desire is to give instead of get, our core belief is that we have so much abundance, we can afford to give it away. The subconscious mind takes its clue from our core beliefs, and brilliantly manufactures situations that reflect them. Our willingness to give directs the universe to give to us.

The miracle worker's goal in every circumstance is peace of mind. *A Course in Miracles* tells us that we don't know what would make us happy; we just think we do. All of us have gotten things we thought would make us happy and they didn't. If we write affirmations for a brown Mercedes-Benz, the power of the subconscious mind is such that we will probably get it. The point is, we won't necessarily be happy once we do. The miracle-minded perception would be to make happiness itself our goal and to relinquish the thought that we know what that would look like. We never know what's going to happen in a month, or a year from now. If we got what we wanted now, then perhaps we would be worse off for it later on.

Let's say you're going in for a job interview. You want the job very much, and someone might have suggested to you that you should affirm you'll be getting the job, making that your goal. But a miracle worker makes peace our only goal. What that does is to direct the mind to focus on all the factors that contribute to our peace, and leave everything else out of our conscious consideration. The mind, like the physical eye, is inundated with so many impressions at one time, that a built-in censor mechanism brings focus to our perception. It chooses what we'll notice and what we won't.

Making our goal anything other than peace is emotionally self-destructive. If our goal is to get the job, then that's fine if we do, but if we don't get the job, we'll feel depressed. If we make peace our goal, then if we get the job, that's great, but if we don't, we're still peaceful.

The Course tells us it's important to set a goal at the beginning of a situation, or it will seem to unfold chaotically. If our goal is peace, we're programmed for emotional stability no matter what happens. The mind will have been directed to see the situation from a peaceful perspective. If we didn't get the job we wanted, it won't matter so much. We will truly understand that there's something better coming up soon, or that this wasn't really the perfect job for us anyway. We will have faith in God. The miracle is that we will really *feel* our faith. It won't just be positive goo thrown over our pain. Our emotions flow from our thoughts, and not the other way around.

Another problem with setting specific goals is that they can be limiting. Perhaps we're asking for something good, when God's will was that we be given something great. Our looking over God's shoulder only interferes with His capacity to make us happy. Once we truly understand that God's will is that we be happy, we no longer feel the need to ask for anything other than that God's will be done.

Once when I was lecturing in New York, a young man stood up and asked me about affirmations. At that time, "Hill Street Blues" was a popular T.V. show. He said, "I've been writing down fifty times before I go to sleep at night, 'I have a regular part on Hill Street Blues, I have a regular part on Hill Street Blues.' Are you telling me I shouldn't do that?"

I said, "You can write those affirmations fifty times before you go to bed at night, and chances are good you'll pull in a part on Hill Street Blues because the mind is very powerful. But for all you know, a year will pass, an important director will be wanting you for the lead in a major feature film, but they won't be able to get you because you're under contract for a little part in Hill Street Blues!"

The issue underlying our need to tell God what to do is our lack of trust. We're afraid to leave things in God's hands because we don't know what He'll do with them. We're afraid He'll lose our file. If we're going to set any goal, let us set the goal of being healed of the belief that God is fear instead of love. Let us remember from the Course that "our happiness and our function are one." If God is our goal, that's the same thing as saying that happiness is our goal. There's no need to believe that God can't figure out the details or provide the ways to make it happen.

8.   *GOD'S PLAN*

"Only God's plan for salvation will work."

Sometimes we carry an attitude at work because we think the job is beneath us, or we resent the fact that other people are the boss and we're not. We're in a hurry to get to the top of the heap. We don't realize that, as we spread love, we climb naturally. Maybe not most quickly, but remember the story of the tortoise and the hare. The tortoise, although he walked slowly and steadily, reached the goal before the quick-footed hare.

"May God's will be done" is the same thing as saying, "May I become the best that I'm capable of being." As we grow in personal stature, we grow into a more responsible energy. People will *want* to hire us, to work with us. Our progress will occur easily. Our success will be an effortless accomplishment. Things will just *happen*. You can have a great resume, but if you have a rotten personality, the going will get rough for you somewhere down the line. A good resume can get you an important interview, but you won't get the job unless they like you.

Much of today's psychological orientation is brittle. It's brittle because everyone is trying so hard, and we're all trying so hard because we think we have to. The way of surrender is like letting God be the sculptor, and letting ourselves be the clay. In the sculpting classes I took in high school, we had to spray the clay with water each day or it would get too dry to work with. That's how we have to be for God: malleable, like moist clay. If we're rigidly attached to getting something, including getting things to work out the way we think they should work out, we are not relaxed. We then have very little room for spontaneous insights.

We never really know why we're going someplace. I have made what I thought were professional contacts that turned out to be personal contacts, and vice versa. In God's world, there's only one work going on, and that's the preparation of His teachers, those who demonstrate love. According to the Course, the Holy Spirit uses any situation given to Him as a lesson in love for everyone involved. But we have to be willing to give up our attachment to a particular outcome in a given situation. We might see a certain project as a vehicle for making money, for instance, and then feel disappointed if it doesn't. We feel confused because we thought we were following the Holy Spirit's guidance in making the effort. But it could be that the real purpose of that particular project was not to make money at all. We do not always know at the time why the Holy Spirit directs us as He does. The miracle worker's function is merely to follow instructions in a desire to serve God. Our compensation, materially and emotionally, will arrive in God's own time and way.

One of the reasons we're always trying to control the results in life is because we think the universe, when left to its own devices, is chaotic. But God is the ultimate order. He is the principle of constantly expanding love in action, in all dimensions, for all life. His power is thoroughly impersonal. He doesn't like some people more than others. He works like a computer. Trusting God is like trusting gravity.

These are important points to remember:

1. God's plan works.
2. Yours doesn't.

As stated by the Course, "I need add nothing to His plan. But to receive it, I must be willing not to substitute my own in place of it. And that is all. Add more, and you will merely take away the little that is asked." It's not our job to figure out how to accomplish God's purposes on earth. That's not help; it's interference. It is merely our job to so deeply align our hearts and minds with His spirit within us, that our lives then become involuntary instruments of His will. Insights occur. Situations shift gear. Our efforts to consciously control the unfolding of good does not produce good so much as it brings forth a slightly less tainted brand of human willfulness.

I have heard it said that living out of our vision is more powerful than living out of our circumstance. Holding on to a vision invokes the circumstances by which the vision is achieved. Vision is content; material circumstances mere form. I have a friend who is running for political office. Having been in politics for many years, his tendency is to think that his political success depends on his being a good politician. But part of the decay of our social order has come about because we are governed by so many people who are politicians rather than leaders. Lyndon Johnson was a great politician but not much of a leader. John Kennedy was a great leader but not much of a politician. The strength of a positive vision for America, through its inspirational effects on all the people who want desperately to see our nation healed, will do more to get someone elected than any amount of conventional politicking. It will touch our hearts.

I told my friend that the key to a successful campaign would be to surrender the campaign to the Holy Spirit and ask that it be used as an instrument of His peace. My friend said that sounded great, but he needed to figure out how to do that. I told him he didn't have to figure out anything. "All you have to do is to be willing," I told him, "and the Holy Spirit will enter where He is invited. You'll be brilliant. You'll be charismatic. Don't try to figure out your message; just ask God what He would have you say. Step back and let Him lead the way."

A silent prayer before every speech and every political appearance would help bring his energies in line with truth. Once I accompanied him to a political rally, and in the car on the way, he shared with me some understand-able judgments of certain people who would be there. "Pray that your perceptions be healed," I said to him as we walked into the building. "Your goal is to lead us into a compassionate society, but you can't give what you don't have. Start by being compassionate towards the people at this rally. As your mind is healed, its ef-fect on others will be automatic. You won't even have to think about what to say. The perfect words will come right out, because love will guide your mind." That's what it would mean to let God run his campaign.

And so it is with any business. Before the meeting, or the interview or the session, or whatever, try saying this prayer:

"Dear God, I surrender this situation to you. May it be used for your purposes. I ask only that my heart be open to give love and to receive love. May all the results unfold according to your will. Amen." Whatever you do, do it for God.

We are strong enough to do any job He asks us to do. Don't be concerned about your own readiness, says the Course, but be consistently aware of His. It is not you doing the work, but the spirit who is within you. Forgetting this causes fear. *A Course in Miracles* says that the presence of fear is a sure sign we're trusting in our own strength. "If you are trusting in your own strength, you have every reason to be apprehensive, anxious and fearful." Of ourselves, none of us have the capacity to work miracles. With the power that is in us but not of us, however, there is nothing we cannot do.

9. SALES TO SERVICE

"Love would always give increase."

When we are motivated by the desire to sell, we are only looking out for ourselves. When we are motivated by the desire to serve, we are looking out for others. Miracles shift us from a sales to a service mentality. Since in the realm of consciousness we only get to keep what we give away, a service mentality is a far more abundant attitude.

The thought system that dominates our culture is laced with selfish values, and relinquishing those values is a lot easier said than done. The journey to a pure heart can be highly disorienting. For years we may have worked for power, money and prestige. Now all of a sudden we've learned that those are just the values of a dying world. We don't know where to search for motivation anymore. If we're not working in order to get rich, then why are we working at all? What are we supposed to do all day? Just sit home and watch T.V.?

Not at all, but thinking so is a temporary phase many people go through—when the values of the old world no longer have a hold on us, but the values of the new don't yet grab your soul. They will. There comes a time, not too long into the journey to God, when the realization that the world could work beautifully if we would give it the chance, begins to excite us. It becomes our new motivation. The news isn't how bad things are. The news is how good they could be. And our own activity could be part of the unfolding of Heaven on earth. There is no more powerful motivation than to feel we're being used in the creation of a world where love has healed all wounds.

We are no longer ambitious for ourselves, but are rather inspired by the vision of a healed world. Inspiration rearranges our energies. It sources within us a new power and direction. We no longer feel like we're trying to carry a football to the finish line, clutching it to our chest and surrounded by hostile forces. We feel instead as though angels are pushing us from behind and making straight our path as we go.

Purity of heart will not make us poor. The exaltation of poverty as a spiritual virtue is of the ego, not the spirit. A person acting from a motivation of contribution and service rises to such a level of moral authority, that worldly success is a natural result.

Give all your gifts away in service to the world. If you want to paint, don't wait for a grant. Paint a wall in your town that looks drab and uninviting. You never know who's going to see that wall. Whatever it is you want to do, give it away in service to your community. At my lectures in Los Angeles, I grew so tired of hearing actors moan about not getting jobs. "Go to hospitals, to retirement homes, to mental institutions," I said. "There was acting before there were acting jobs. If you want to act, *act*." Some people who heard me formed a group called the Miracle Players, and they did just that.

"I don't want to do it because I can't make a living doing it," is a very weak beam to send into the universe. I lectured on *A Course in Miracles* for at least two years before it became the source of my income. When I started lecturing, I had no idea it would become my profession. Some things you do for no other reason than because they're the right thing to do. "I'll do this because it serves, even if I'm not paid," is a very high beam. It says to the universe that you must be very serious. And when you get serious about the universe, the universe gets serious about you.

I never felt the need to advertise much for my lectures. I figured if they were of genuine interest to people, then people would hear about them. That's not to say that advertising is bad, as long as the motivation for advertising is to inform people as opposed to manipulating them. Arnold Patent wrote that if you genuinely have something to say, there is someone who genuinely needs to hear it. We don't have to invent an audience so much as we have to hone the message we plan to give them once they get here. Serving three people is as important as serving three hundred. Once we're clear about how to deal with a small following, a large following will develop automatically, if that would serve the world. Our power lies in our clarity about the role our work can play in the creation of a more beautiful world. The miracle is to think of our career as our contribution, however small, to the healing of the universe.

The ego's world is based on finite resources, but God's world is not. In God's world, which is the real world, the more we give, the more we have. Our having a piece of the world's pie doesn't mean there's less for anyone else, and someone else having a piece of the pie doesn't mean there's less for us. So we needn't compete, in business or anywhere else. Our generosity towards others is key to our positive experience of the world. There's enough room for everyone to be beautiful. There's enough room for everyone to be successful. There's enough room for everyone to be rich. It is only our thinking that blocks that possibility from happening.

The people who have achieved more than you, in any area, are only a half step ahead of you in time. Bless them and praise their gifts, and bless and praise your own. The world would be less rich without their contributions, and it would be less rich without yours. There's more than room for everyone; in fact, there's a need for everyone.

As we are healed, the world is healed. Doing anything for a purpose other than love means reliving the split from God, perpetuating and maintaining that split. Every person is a cell in the body of human consciousness. At the moment, it is as though the body of Christ is suffering from cancer. In cancer, a normal working cell decides that it no longer wants to function in contribution to the whole. Instead of being part of the support system of the blood or the liver, the cell goes off and builds its own kingdom. That's a malignancy, which threatens to destroy the organism.

So it is with the body of humanity. Everyone's gone off to do their own thing: *my* career, *my* store, *my* money. We've lost sight of our essential interrelatedness, and this forgetfulness threatens to destroy us. The "my" mentality is the ego. It is the belief in separation. It is the cosmic disease. Taking what we have and devoting it to the restoration of the whole is our salvation and the salvation of the world. Our devotion then becomes our work, and our work becomes our devotion.

CHAPTER 8

The Body

*"The body was not made by love. Yet love
does not condemn it and can use it lovingly,
respecting what the Son of God has made and
using it to save him from illusions."*

1.   THE BODY'S PURPOSE

"Let the body have healing as its purpose."

In the world of bodies, we are all separate. In the world of spirit, we are all one. Citing the Course, we heal the separation between the two by shifting our awareness from body identification to spirit identification. This heals the body as well as the mind.

We think we're separate because we have bodies, when in truth, we have bodies because we think we're separate. The Course says that the body is "a tiny fence around a little part of a glorious and complete idea." But that doesn't mean the body is bad. Like everything else within the world of form, the mind ascribes to it either fearful or loving purposes. The ego's use of the body is to maintain the illusion of separation: The ego uses the body for attack, pleasure and pride. The Holy Spirit's use of the body is to heal that illusion: "In this sense, the body does become a temple to God; His voice abides in it by directing the use to which it is put."

The body's holiness lies in its potential for communication. When given to the Holy Spirit, the body becomes "a beautiful lesson in communion which has value until communion *is*." The Holy Spirit asks us to give Him our hands, our feet, our voices, in order that He might use them as instruments for saving the world. To see the body as a means by which the world is transformed, and not an end in itself, is a healthy perception of the body. To see the body as an end instead of a means, to ascribe to it selfish or unloving purposes, is to put a burden on the body that the body was never meant to carry. This is sick thinking, which produces sickness in the body.

Living on this earth, we have learned to see ourselves as bodies. An individual body is physically small and vulnerable in relation to the rest of the universe, and so, since we think we are bodies, we experience ourselves as small and vulnerable. Living within the realization that we are much more than bodies, that we are spirits within the mind of God, expands the level of our awareness and places us outside the limitations of ordinary physical law. This correction of our perception, this Atonement, is our healing. It is not the body that gets sick, but the mind. As shown in the Course, health or sickness of the body "depends entirely on how the mind perceives it, and the purpose that the mind would use it for." It is not the body but the mind that is in need of healing, and the only healing is a return to love.

Our bodies are merely blank canvases onto which we project our thoughts. Disease is loveless thinking materialized. This doesn't mean that people who have contracted a disease thought lovelessly, while the rest of us didn't. Great saints have contracted terminal illnesses. The lovelessness that manufactures disease is systemic; it is laced throughout racial consciousness. Which soul manifests illness is based on many factors.

Let's say an innocent child dies of environmentally-based cancer. How was lovelessness the problem here? The loveless thinking was not necessarily in the child, but in many of us who, over the years, lived without reverence for the environment, allowing it to be polluted by toxic chemicals. The child's physical sickness resulted, indirectly, from the sickness in someone else's mind. Our loving thoughts affect people and situations we never even dream of, and so do our mistakes. Since our minds do not stop at our brain casings—since there is no place where one mind stops and another starts—then our love touches everyone, and so does our fear.

A healthy perception of our bodies is one in which we surrender them to the Holy Spirit and ask that they be used as instruments through which love is expressed into the world. The Course states, "The body is merely part of your experience in the physical world. . . . [It] is nothing more than a framework for developing abilities, which is quite apart from what they are used for." *A Course in Miracles* says that "health is the result of relinquishing all attempts to use the body lovelessly." The use of the body for any other purpose than the extension of love is diseased thinking. It is at odds with our natural knowingness and the conflict it engenders is reflected in our physical as well as our mental states.

2.   HEALTH AND HEALING

"The body is not the source of its own health."

A friend of mine told me that we're not punished *for* our sins, but *by* our sins. Sickness is not a sign of God's judgment on us, but of our judgment on ourselves. If we were to think that God created our sickness, how could we turn to Him for healing? As we've already established, God is all that is good. He creates only love, therefore he did not create sickness. Sickness is an illusion and does not actually exist. It is part of our worldly dream, our self-created nightmare. Our prayer to God is that He awaken us from the dream.

When any of us awaken, the entire world is brought closer to Heaven. In asking for healing, we are not just asking for our own health, but rather we are asking that the idea of sickness be removed from the mind of God's Son. As shown in *A Course in Miracles*, "If the mind can heal the body, but the body cannot heal the mind, then the mind must be stronger than the body." Forgiveness is the ultimate preventative medicine as well as the greatest healer. We heal the body by remembering that it is not who we really are. We are spirits and not bodies, we are eternally healthy and we are incapable of sickness. These are merely statements of the truth about ourselves, and it is always truth that sets us free.

Illness is a sign of separation from God, and healing is a sign that we have returned to Him. The return to God is merely the return to love. In his book *Quantum Healing*, Dr. Deepak Chopra tells a powerful story about the connection between love and physical healing:

> *An Ohio University study of heart disease in the 1970s was conducted by feeding quite toxic, high-cholesterol diets to rabbits in order to block their arteries, duplicating the effect that such a diet has on human arteries. Consistent results began to appear in all the rabbit groups except for one, which strangely displayed 60 percent fewer symptoms. Nothing in the rabbits' physiology could account for their high tolerance to the diet, until it was discovered by accident that the student who was in charge of feeding these particular rabbits liked to fondle and pet them. He would hold each rabbit lovingly for a few minutes before feeding it; astonishingly, this alone seemed to enable the animals to overcome the toxic diet. Repeat experiments, in which one group of rabbits was treated neutrally while the others were loved, came up with similar results. Once again, the mechanism that causes such*

immunity is quite unknown—it is baffling to think that evolution has built into the rabbit mind an immune response that needs to be triggered by human cuddling.

Studies have shown that cancer patients who attend support groups live, on the average, twice as long after diagnosis as those who don't. What is this "psycho-immunological factor" which, by now, science knows exists, but doesn't know how to identify? That factor is love, or God.

God is of no practical value if we perceive Him merely as a free-floating concept, divorced from the power of physical expression. It is only when He is expressed on the earth, His love channeled through human beings as in the case of the student cuddling the rabbits, or support groups where the space is created for increased compassion and understanding, that He is allowed to penetrate the veil of human darkness.

Over the last several years I have counseled many people diagnosed with cancer, AIDS and other life-challenging illnesses. In 1987, I asked my friend Louise Hay if she would help me start a nonprofit organization dedicated to helping people in physical crisis, to be called The Los Angeles Center for Living. In 1989, The Manhattan Center for Living opened in New York City. The Centers' mission statement is that we provide free nonmedical support services to people dealing with life-challenging illness and grief. On both coasts, we have seen the miracles that occur when people invoke the power of love in the midst of disease and grief.

"Do not look to the god of sickness for healing but only to the God of love," says the Course, "for healing is the acknowledgement of Him." In the traditional Western medical model, a healer's job is to attack disease. But if the consciousness of attack is the ultimate problem, how could it be the ultimate answer? A miracle worker's job is not to attack illness, but rather to stimulate the natural forces of healing. We turn our eyes away from sickness to the love that lies beyond it. No sickness can diminish our capacity to love.

Does that mean that it is a mistake to take medicine? Absolutely not. *A Course in Miracles* reminds us that the Holy Spirit enters into our lives at our present level of consciousness. Many of us believe that the doctor in the white coat can heal us with that pill he's giving us. Therefore, says the Course, we should take the pill. But the healing doesn't come from the pill. It comes from our belief.

Cancer studies have shown that rates of recovery in patients choosing traditional medical treatment, versus those taking a more holistic route, are roughly equal. This makes perfect sense, because in neither case is the recovery a result of the form of cure. It is the patient's mental and emotional interaction with his treatment that activates its healing power.

I have led support groups for people dealing with life-challenging illness, where during the entire session, disease was mentioned only in passing. We attend groups not to grow closer to our disease, but rather to grow closer to the power for healing which lies within us. Many of the issues that confront us when we are ill are the same issues that confronted us in one way or another when we were still healthy, but we didn't deal with them until now. Life goes on when we are ill. It is merely intensified. We tend to handle illness basically the way we handle everything else in life. We must avoid the temptation to see illness as a block to our capacity to find God, and instead use it as a springboard from which we soar into His arms.

3.   HEALTHY THINKING

"Healing, then, is a way of approaching knowledge by thinking in accordance with the laws of God."

There is a healing force within each of us, a kind of divine physician seated within our minds and in communication with every cell of our being. This force is the intelligence that drives the immune system. Its presence is obvious to us whenever we cut a finger or break a leg.

What is this "divine intelligence" and how is it activated? The Atonement releases the mind to its full creative power. "Jesus saves" means "love heals the mind." How did Jesus heal the leper? By forgiving him. He stood in the midst of illusion and yet saw only the truth as God created it. He healed through corrected perception. When he stood in front of a leper, he didn't see leprosy. He extended his perception beyond what the physical senses revealed, to reality as seen through the vision of the Holy Spirit. Within the leper is the Son of God, perfect, unalterable, changeless. The spirit is eternally healthy. The spirit cannot get sick and the spirit cannot die.

Jesus sees only as God sees. He accepted the Atonement for himself. Jesus did not *believe* in leprosy. Since all minds are connected, in his presence the leper no longer believed in it either. And so the leper was healed.

In *A Course in Miracles*, Jesus, who is the personal symbol of the Holy Spirit, says, "Your mind and mine can unite in shining your ego away." Asking the Holy Spirit to heal us when we are sick means asking him to heal the thoughts within us which give rise to sickness.

Several years ago, when I had just begun lecturing on *A Course in Miracles*, I had a series of three car accidents in which I was rear-ended on the freeway. In every case, I had surrendered the experience immediately, remembering that I was not subject to the effect of worldly danger, and was not harmed or hurt in any way.

A week or so after the last accident, I developed a cold and a serious sore throat. On a Friday afternoon, with a lecture to give about the Course the next morning, I was feeling terrible. I had a date for drinks after work with my girlfriend Sarah. Since I felt so bad I wanted to cancel the date and go home to bed, but when I called Sarah's office I was told that she had already left for the day. I had no choice but to go to the café, and on my way driving there, I turned my attention to healing my throat. I wished desperately for access to a doctor, because I knew that an antibiotic called Erythromycin had always healed this throat problem for me in the past. Since I was new in Los Angeles, I didn't know any doctors yet. I turned to the Course. How did this happen, I asked myself. Where did my thinking deviate from truth? Where was my wrong-minded perception? I received the answer as soon as I asked, and it struck me like a bolt of lightning. Although I had applied principle in relation to the accident itself, I had "given into temptation" right afterwards. In what way? After three accidents, everyone I knew had come up to ask me if I was all right. They put their hands on me, rubbed my neck and back gently, inquired as to whether I'd seen a doctor, and oozed gentleness all over me. *The attention felt good. Being sick made people love me more.* Instead of responding with a full tilt, "I'm fine," the "I'm fine" came out a little more timidly, lest they'd stop rubbing my neck. I had bought into—entered into agreement with—the idea of my physical vulnerability in order to receive the payoff of love and attention.

I paid a high price for my "sin," i.e. loveless perception. My perception was wrong-minded in the sense that I saw myself as a body rather than a spirit, which is a loveless rather than loving self-identification. Choosing to believe I was vulnerable, even for an instant, made me so. Thus my sore throat.

Great, I thought. I got it! "God," I said. "I totally understand how this happened. I return my mind to the point of my error, and I atone. I go back. I ask that my perception be healed, and I ask to be released from the effects of my wrong-minded thinking. Amen." I closed my eyes at a red light while I said the prayer, and fully expected to be free of my sore throat when I opened them again.

The prayer over, I opened my eyes. My throat still hurt. This wasn't supposed to happen. Now more depressed than ever, I went into the café where I was to meet my friend and took a seat at the bar. I noticed as I entered that there was a man at the other end of the bar, looking at me in a flirtatious kind of way. He was anything but my type. I looked at him as though to say, "One more look my direction, buddy, and you're dead."

"Can I help you?" asked the bartender.

"Yes," I whispered hoarsely. "I want some brandy, some honey and some milk."

The man at the other end of the bar watched as the bartender returned with the items I'd requested. "What are you trying to do?" he asked.

I did not want to speak to this man. I wanted him to go away. But once the Course has gotten into your system, you never again have guilt-free bitchy thoughts. "He's your brother, Marianne," I said to myself. "He's an innocent child of God. *Be nice.*"

I softened. "I'm trying to make a hot toddy," I said. "I have a very bad sore throat."

"Well first of all, that's not the way to make a hot toddy," he said, "and secondly, that's not what you want anyway. You probably need some penicillin."

"That's true, I do," I said, "Erythromycin would cure this but I just moved to L.A. and I don't know any doctors who would prescribe it to me."

The man got up and walked over to where I was sitting. He put a credit card on the bar and beckoned the bartender. "Come on, let's go next door," he said to me. "I can get you some Erythromycin."

I looked at him like he was crazy, but I also noticed that the credit card said "Dr." on it. "What's next door?" I asked.

"A Thrifty drugstore."

And so it was. We walked next door to Thrifty and my new friend the doctor prescribed the medicine I wanted. After throwing one pill into my mouth, I became ecstatic.

"You don't understand," I said to him, practically jumping up and down. "*This is a miracle!* I prayed for healing, and I corrected my thoughts but the Holy Spirit couldn't give me an instantaneous healing because I'm not advanced enough yet to receive it—it would be too threatening to my belief system—so He had to enter at the level of my understanding, and you were there, but if I hadn't opened my heart to you I would never have been able to receive the miracle because I wouldn't have been open!"

He handed me his business card. "Young lady, here's my number," he said. "I'm a psychiatrist and I haven't prescribed an antibiotic in twenty-five years. But trust me, you should give me a call."

As I told the good doctor, I asked that my misperceptions be healed—I accepted the Atonement—but the healing could still only enter at the level of my receptivity. The Course tells us that the Holy Spirit steps aside in the presence of fear. Most of us, were we to have a broken leg healed instantly upon hearing the word Jesus, would find the healing more depressing than the wound. That's because, if such a thing is possible, the entire world is something other than we think it is. Giving up our limited understanding of the world, which we experience as a kind of pseudo-control, is more of a threat to us than a broken leg. Some people, says *A Course in Miracles*, would rather die than change their minds. The Holy Spirit finds ways to express His power through vehicles we can accept. Medicine is such a vehicle.

There is a saying in Alcoholics Anonymous that "Every problem comes bearing its own solution." Crisis comes bearing its solution in that it takes us to our knees, our most humble thinking. If we had been there to begin with—if we had placed the power of God before our own, putting love before all personal ambitions—then our problems would not have developed.

An epidemic such as AIDS is a collective heartbreak, pulling millions of people into its painful vortex. But this also means that it brings millions of people to their knees. As soon as enough of us get there, as soon as love reaches a critical mass or, as the Course says, enough people become miracle-minded, there will be a sudden breakthrough in consciousness—a rapture, an instantaneous healing. It will be as though millions of us are stopped at that red light, recognizing our lovelessness and asking that we be healed. When the cure for AIDS is finally found, we will give prizes to a few scientists, but many of us will know that millions and millions of prayers helped it happen.

4. *SAVING THE MIND, SAVING THE BODY*

"Only salvation can be said to cure."

The experience of illness is a call to a genuinely religious life. In that sense, it is for many people one of the best things that ever happened to them.

One of the problems with illness is that it strongly tempts us to obsess about the body at the very time when we need most to concentrate on spirit. It takes spiritual discipline to turn that around. Spiritual practice is mental and emotional exercise, not unlike physical exercise in the way it works. Through spiritual work we are seeking to rebuild our mental musculature. We achieve so little, says *A Course in Miracles*, because we have undisciplined minds. Training our minds to think from a loving, faithful perspective is the greatest boost we can give to our immune systems, and one of the greatest challenges we can pose to our minds.

Changing our lives can be difficult. For a person who has been diagnosed with a physical ailment, the call to change is imperative. Where we used to eat unhealthy foods, we must now eat healthy ones. Where we used to smoke, drink, or get too little sleep, we must now change those habits. And where our minds used to run instinctively in the directions of fear, paranoia and attack, we must now do everything possible to train our minds to think differently.

The body-mind connection might be new to Western science, but it is not new to Eastern medicine, or to the fields of religion and philosophy. The body has an intelligence of its own. As Deepak Chopra writes in *Quantum Healing*, "Life itself is intelligence riding everywhere on chemicals. We mustn't make the mistake of thinking that the rider and the horse are the same." In the traditional Western model of healing, we are trying to get the horse to move in a new direction, without considering having a conversation with the horse's driver. A spiritual, holistic notion of healing includes treatment not only of the body, but of the mind and spirit as well. As Chopra writes, "We have ultimately arrived at a dramatic shift in world view. For the first time in the history of science, mind has a visible scaffold to stand upon. Before this, science declared that we are physical machines that somehow learned to think. Now it dawns that we are thoughts that have learned to create a physical machine."

Love changes the way we think about our disease. Illness comes from separation, says *A Course in Miracles*, and healing comes from joining. Of course people hate their cancer, or hate their AIDS, but the last thing a sick person needs is something else to hate about themselves. Healing results from a transformed perception of our relationship to illness, one in which we respond to the problem with love instead of fear. When a child presents a cut finger to his or her mother, the woman doesn't say, "Bad cut." Rather, she kisses the finger, showers it with love in an unconscious, instinctive activation of the healing process. Why should we think differently about critical illness? Cancer and AIDS and other serious illnesses are physical manifestations of a psychic scream, and their message is not "Hate me," but "Love me."

If I'm yelling, the person in front of me can react in one of two ways. He can yell back, screaming at me to shut up, but this will tend to make me scream more. Or he can tell me that he cares what my feelings are and he loves me and is sorry that I'm feeling this way, which will tend to quiet me down. Those are our two choices with critical illness. Attacking disease is not a cure. Attacking a disease only makes it yell louder. Healing comes from entering into a conversation with our illness, seeking to understand what it's trying to tell us. The physician seeks to understand the chemical alphabet through which illness speaks. The metaphysician seeks to understand what the illness is trying to say.

Lucifer is seen to have been the most beautiful angel in Heaven before he "fell." In *Star Wars*, Darth Vader turns out to have been a nice guy at an earlier time. Disease is love turned into fear—our own energy, meant to sustain us, turned against ourselves. Energy cannot be destroyed. Our job is not to kill disease, but to turn its energy back in the direction it came from—to turn fear back into love.

Visualization has become a popular technique for the treatment of critical illnesses. People often visualize a PAC-MAN, or soldier with a machine gun, setting out to destroy the threatening cells or virus. But we can take a more loving approach. Underneath Darth Vader's ugly mask lay a real man with a real heart. AIDS, for instance, can be thought of as "Angels-In-Darth Vader-Suits."

Here are some enlightened visualizations: Imagine the AIDS virus as Darth Vader, and then unzip his suit to allow an angel to emerge. See the cancer cell or AIDS virus in all its wounded horror, and then see a golden light, or angel, or Jesus, enveloping the cell and transforming it from darkness into light. As we said before, a scream responds best to love. That is when it calms down. That is when it stops.

I have used an interesting letter-writing technique in my work, where people write a letter to AIDS or cancer or whatever illness they might have, and tell it everything they feel. The letter begins,

for instance:

Dear Cancer,
These are my honest feelings.
. . . . .
. . . . .
Signed,
Ed

And then we wrote a letter back, to Ed from AIDS.

Dear Ed,
These are my honest feelings.
. . . . .
. . . . .
Signed,
AIDS

The following letters were written in one of my AIDS workshops:

Dear AIDS,
I used to hate you. I was confused and
afraid to accept the idea of death and sickness.
I believed the newsprint and TV, doctors, and
all of that fear that others tried to lay into me
on a daily basis. However, today I find I'm
not dead three and a half years later, and even
with all these medical problems, I'm more alive
today than ever. I'm a grown-up thanks to your
appearance in my life. You've given me a reason

to live and I love you for it. My friends are sick or dead but I'm not them. I'm me. And I do not feel threatened or afraid of something that was once an enemy and has now become my strength.

Steve

Dear Steve,

If I was, as they say, out to get you, don't you think you'd be dead by now? I'm not able to kill, harm, or make you sick. I have no brain, brute strength or great harming force. I'm just a virus. You give me the power you should give to God. I take what I can because I don't want to die any more than you do. Yes, I live off your fears. But I die from your peace of mind, serenity, honesty, faith and desire to live.

Sincerely,

The AIDS virus

Dear AIDS,

I am so afraid of dying young. I am so afraid of going to the hospital and having all these needles and things stuck in me. I am so afraid of pain. Why do you have to do this to me and my friends? What did we ever do to make you mad at us and want to hurt us? If there is something you are trying to tell us, can't you tell us in a different way? I miss my friends. Why did you have to kill them? Why did you have to cause them such physical pain? Sometimes I'm so angry at you but right now I'm not angry. I'm just sad. I'm confused. I don't know what to do to calm you down. So far you've left me alone, but why, and for how long? John is such a gentle person. Why must he suffer? If it's love you want, we can love you. If you have any doubts, look at the love surrounding this disease. Please answer soon. Tell us what you want. I feel like we don't have much time but I'm willing to listen and learn. Thank you.

Carl

Dear Carl,

   I don't understand this any better than you do. I don't mean you and your loved ones any harm. I'm just trying to exist, just like you, doing it in the best way I know how. Unfortunately, it ends up hurting people. I just want love, just like you do. I'm crying out but no one seems to hear me. Maybe if we try listening to each other and talking to each other, we can find a way to exist in peace without hurting each other. Right now, I feel like you only want to destroy me rather than dealing with whatever it is inside of you that brought me here. Please don't hate me and try to destroy me. Love me.

Let's talk and listen to each other and try to live in peace. Thanks.

AIDS

Dear HIV,

A little over eleven years ago you blew into town. Everything has changed since that time. Many people have left because of you. I really miss them a lot. There has been so much pain and suffering because of you. On a conscious level, no one wanted you. I myself have been personally dealing with you too long already. Back in '87 and '88, you almost took me out. I just thought you might like to know that it is 1991 now and I'm still around and so are you. Isn't it about time we stop this bullshit and become friends? Let's put the past behind us and grow forward together. I have tried to love you as best I can, but sometimes I really have difficulty doing so. Please, let's be friends and make up.

Love always,

Paul

Dear Paul,
   Okay.
   Love,

HIV

Dear AIDS,

I'm really pissed off! Why do I have to
worry about you and death when I'm only 26?
I want to know I'll be alive for my ten-year
class reunion, but no—it's a big maybe. I'm
also sick of worrying that every cold I get or
sleep pattern that's different is a sign of the end
coming. I'm tired of worrying about others
finding out. Get out of my body. I don't want
you here! That's all.

Russ

Dear Russ,

Both you and I don't know how we came to
be, but we're here together. I would be glad to
go, but that door is not open to me. Hey, I've
given you a perspective on life and death most
people your age never think about! Work with
me, we'll get through this.

AIDS

Dear AIDS,

I, like lots of other people, have been
through so much pain and so many changes,
both physically and mentally. Now, yes, there
is a great part inside me who is very angry and
sad. It feels like a big nightmare. Yes, I must
have done something to cause this disease. But
what a wound to be punished like this. I must

say, I do not like all the pain I've gone through with this crazy disease, and I don't like the suffering it has put me through mentally. But I pray daily.

Peter

Dear Peter,

I'm in your body and yes I am a virus and yes I have caused you a great deal of discomfort. But I do assure you that the power of your mind does make a difference. You know if it did not, you would not be here. Yes, I have altered your life in some ways, but in some ways positively. Your mind is much more powerful than I am.

AIDS

Dear AIDS,

I hate the uncertainty. But I feel thankful for the kick in the butt this was in my life, and to those around me. You made me find the strength I always had, and made me see the love those around me could show. You made us all learn to appreciate every day and the strength I was capable of. I know I keep saying strength, but it's true, AIDS gave me strength. This is because when you find out your biggest fear in life comes true and you can still move on, fear no longer has any strength. Thank you for helping me stop beating up on myself and hating what I wasn't, and making me love what I am.

Andrew

Dear Andrew,
    You're welcome.

AIDS

Dear AIDS virus,
    Go to Hell. You took a shining star from my family. I miss him and loved him and I never told him. Why do you invade us in our prime? Why do you strike with such vengeance? I hate the pain and agony you cause, but somehow you brought out the best in Leo and the best in his family.

Inez

Dear Inez,
    I didn't bring out the worst or best. I just am. And how you live with me is up to each of you.

AIDS

I suggest to every person dealing with a serious illness in themselves or others, that they consider starting a journal in which they "communicate" with their illness. Seeing sickness as our own love that needs to be reclaimed, is a more positive approach to healing than is seeing the sickness as something hideous we must get rid of. Energy cannot be destroyed. It can, however, be miraculously transformed. That miracle emerges from our own thoughts, our own decision to let go our belief in fear and danger, and to embrace instead, a view of the world that is based on hope and love. There is certainly nothing to lose, no risk in trying. "The Atonement is so gentle you need but whisper to it and all its power will rush to your assistance and support." God does His part when we do ours.

5.   THE BODY IN RELATIONSHIPS

"The body does not separate you from your brother, and if you think it does you are insane."

Our real identity lies not in our body, but in our spirit. "The Christ in you inhabits not a body," says the Course. Neither is another person's body who they really are, either. The body is an illusionary wall that appears to separate us, the ego's chief device in trying to convince us that we are separate from each other and separate from God.

The Course calls the body "the central figure in the dreaming of the world." The human storyline, where bodies talk and move and suffer and die, forms a veil of unreality in front of God's creation. It hides "the face of Christ." My brother might lie, but he is not that lie. My brothers might fight, but they remain joined in love.

"Minds are joined," says the Course, but "bodies are not." The body of itself is nothing. It cannot forgive, it cannot see, and it cannot communicate. "If you choose to see the body you behold a world of separation, unrelated things, and happenings that make no sense at all."

"When you equate yourself with a body, you will always experience depression," says the Course. Equating another person with a body will bring up the same anxiety. One of the ways the body can be used to manufacture depression is through loveless sex. Our sexual impulses become canvases onto which we extend our love or project our fear. When sex is of the Holy Spirit, it is a deepening of communication. When it is of the ego, it is a substitute for communication. The Holy Spirit uses sex to heal us; the ego uses it to wound us. Sometimes we have thought that sex with another person would cement the bond between us, and instead it turned out to manufacture more illusion and anxiety than there was before. It is only when sex is a vehicle for spiritual communion that it is truly loving, that it joins us to another person. Then it is a sacred act.

Holiness means the presence of a loving purpose, and in that sense, the body and its accouterments can be a holy expression. Many spiritual seekers have felt the need to eschew all body-related things. But that can actually be as ego-centered as an overattachment to the physical. Anything used to spread joy and communicate love is a part of God's plan for salvation.

When I was about twenty years old, I had my first date with a man in a suit. I had never before been picked up at my house by a man wearing anything but blue-jeans. When I opened the door and saw a handsome man in a suit and a beautiful overcoat, my first thought was that maybe he was in the mafia!

I went on the date and struggled for the entire evening with my conflicts about his wardrobe. I couldn't tell this man, of course, that I was turned off by his gorgeous clothes! He was an Italian, and my first exposure to a European man's sensibilities towards women. Years later I would remember what this man taught me.

We started dating, and I had never known someone to make such a fuss over me. He treated our nights out like major events. Did I wish to see a play or a movie? Did I want to go to this restaurant, or that? What should he wear? I was so surprised by what a big deal it was to him, whether he wore the blue shirt or the white. At first it annoyed me, coming as I was from a sixties mentality that viewed all such considerations as irrelevant. But I ultimately saw that the central issue for him was that he wished to make me happy. His dressing up was a way to please me, a way of communicating how much he cared.

Many years after that relationship, I was walking through a clothing store with a boyfriend. He was looking at two jackets, and couldn't decide which one to buy. When I indicated which I liked, he acted almost as though I was his mother—he would prove to me that my opinion wouldn't dictate his decision. I said to him, "That's the difference between you and me. If I were buying clothes, your liking something would make me more prone to buy it. What's the point of being in a relationship with you if it doesn't motivate me to try to please you, to make your life more pleasurable, to sweeten things for you?"

That's the only purpose for make-up, or clothes, or anything else in the world of form. Their point is not to seduce another person, but to add light to the world in the form of beauty and pleasure. The meaning in things is how much we use them to contribute happiness to the world. Clothes and other personal effects are no different than any other art form. If we perceive them lovingly, they can lift the vibrations and increase the energy in the world around us.

This is not narcissism or vanity. Our *not* caring whether the boyfriend or husband, girlfriend or wife really likes the outfit—that's the narcissism. I have had boyfriends who were as adamant that they preferred me without make-up, as others have been that they wanted me always to wear it. The change for me has had nothing to do with what kind of men I dated, but with a shift from "I don't care what he wants," to "I care very much what makes him happy." The first part of the sexual revolution entailed women breaking from the oppressive patterns of subservience to men. The second part entails our recognition that there is no point in developing individuality except to then surrender it to a higher identity. And the highest identity is our relationship with others. A life lived for oneself alone is not liberation, but merely another form of bondage. Since we are not bodies, we do not exist in isolation. Living as though we do can only lead to pain.

6.   VANITY, WEIGHT AND AGE

"The eyes of the body see only form."

What is vanity? What is the ego-oriented, neurotic obsession with weight, hair, looks, and sex appeal that drives Americans to spend billions of dollars a year on products they can't afford and don't really need, and young women to fall into dangerous disease patterns in their efforts to be thin? These things are inevitable results of a cultural orientation that leaves out the reality of spirit. Concentration on the body as an end rather than a means in our perception, breeds fear. Fear that we're not good enough or attractive enough. Fear that they won't like us. Fear that we'll lose out in life. There is no way to escape this painful maelstrom without replacing body identification with the memory that we aren't bodies at all, that who we are is the love inside us, and it is that love alone that determines our value. When our minds are filled with light, there is no room for darkness. When we understand who and what we really are, there is no room for pain and confusion.

When I was in my twenties, I had a problem with weight—not enough of a problem to be called fat, but enough to keep me miserable. There was a problematic ten to fifteen pounds that I could never shake. Anytime I went on a diet, I ended up gaining weight. This makes sense psychologically, because if someone tells us not to think about the Eiffel Tower, we'll think about it all the time. Telling myself not to think about food only made me more obsessed about it. Deprivation is a lousy way to lose weight. I used to pray about my problem and would receive the following guidance: "Eat anything you want." That sounded thoroughly insane to me. "But if I tell myself to do that," I thought, "then I'll start eating and I'll never stop." To that my internal guidance responded, "Yes, you will do that at first. You will have to compensate for all the pressure you've been putting on yourself for years. And then you will have had enough. Then you will return to your natural rhythms. Then you will heal."

So I let go. I met a woman who had lost a huge amount of weight and told me she had asked God to do it for her. "I didn't ask that I lose weight," she said. "I just asked that he take the monkey off my back. I didn't even care if I was fat. I told Him that if He wanted me to be fat, to make me comfortable with it. I just wanted out of this hell."

I decided that it didn't matter how much I weighed.

I couldn't take the horror of the obsession anymore. Becoming a student of *A Course in Miracles*, I began to realize that how much I weighed didn't matter. All that mattered was love. If I could train my mind to concentrate more on that, then my problems would disappear by themselves. In the Eastern religions it is often said, "Go for God, and all that is not authentically you will drop." As I got more involved with practicing the Course, I stopped thinking so much about my weight. That was all. And one day I looked in the mirror and saw that it was gone.

What I realized was that my weight had nothing to do with my body, but with my mind. I was terrified of people, and had unconsciously manufactured a wall around myself to protect me from them. I was terrified, however, because of the love that I myself was not giving. My ego's purpose for the weight was to keep me separate, and until I gave up that purpose, I would never be able to give up the extra pounds. My subconscious mind was merely following instructions. As I began to put my energy into reaching across the wall, when I allowed the Christ to enter my mind, the wall miraculously disappeared.

After learning in the Course that the body isn't important, I couldn't understand why we should exercise or eat well. What I learned was that, when I exercise, I actually think less about my body than when I don't. When I don't exercise, I can't help thinking about heavy thighs and a thick waist. Similarly, the point of healthy food is that it supports us in existing the most lightly and energetically within the body. It is heavier, unhealthy food that ties us to the body. We take care of the body as a way of taking better care of the spirit.

As we exist today, an aging body reflects the heaviness of our pained and worried thoughts. As we begin to travel more lightly within the body, and our minds give up our constant preoccupation with body thoughts, aging becomes a different experience. I read somewhere that the Virgin Mary never aged, although she lived into her fifties. I can see why. If we were to achieve a state in which only love and caring filled our minds, and neither past nor future lay as burdens on our shoulders, aging would become a youthing process. Spiritually, we should be getting younger the older we get, since the only purpose of time is that we learn to more consistently relinquish our attachment to form. Then the body springs into perfect life, a healthy instrument and a thing of joy.

Part of our cultural neurosis has been an abhorrence of age. Like anything else, age will only transform when we have first accepted it as it is. Many of us think age is so terrible, so unappealing, so unsexy, when actually those are just thoughts we have. Walking down the street in Paris, French women in their fifties and sixties exude a mature sexuality. Here, we tend to hold the thought that women that age are "over the hill."

Let's change our minds. Let's remember that the longer we live, the more we know, and the more we know, the more beautiful we are. We can actively create a new context for the experience of aging by shifting our outlook towards older people in our society. The ego, after all, claims that a diminished body is a diminished person. We are a cold and uncaring culture in our treatment of older Americans. In China, elders are respected and revered, which is a large part of why the Chinese live so long as healthy, productive citizens. We have a thought in America that youth is better, and so it is. Not because that is an objective truth, but only because it is a thought we carry and manifest as our collective experience.

No matter what the illness or addiction or distorted physical expression, its cause is in the mind, and only there can it be healed. The greatest power we're given, says the Course, is the power to change our mind. Our physical condition does not determine our emotional condition. The experience of peace comes only from the mind. "Peace of mind," says *A Course in Miracles*, "is clearly an internal matter."

7. THE MEANING OF HEALING

"Forget not that the healing of God's Son is all the world is for."

When we think of healing, we usually think of physical healing, but *A Course in Miracles* defines health as "inner peace." There are people experiencing critical illness who are at peace, and people in perfect physical health who are emotionally tortured.

In his book *Teach Only Love*, Jerry Jampolsky sets forth his principles of attitudinal healing. He teaches that peace is possible regardless of physical circumstances. In surrendering our illness to God, we surrender the experience in its entirety, knowing that anything can be used by the Holy Spirit to bring more love into our awareness.

Many people have spoken of their illnesses as a "wake-up call." That means wake up and experience life—wake up and bless each morning, wake up and appreciate friends and family. I have heard people with critical illnesses say that their lives only really began when they were diagnosed. Why is that? Because whenever we are diagnosed with a critical illness, much of our superficial personal baggage is dropped in the first five minutes. Why do I act so arrogantly? Why I am pretending to be so tough? Why am I judging so many people? Why am I not appreciating all the love and beauty that surrounds me? Why am I avoiding the simplest and most important element of my being, the love in my heart?

Dropping our illusions is a healing in itself. Within each of us there is a core—our essence, our true being. That is the place of God who is within us. Finding that essence is our return to God. It is the purpose of our lives, and even our most painful experiences can serve that purpose.

Over the years, I have officiated at many funerals and memorial services. Some of the most impressive sights I have ever seen have been the grieving faces of people confronting a naked truth that cannot be denied or shoved away. When someone we love is no longer with us, our sadness opens us to new opportunities for growth. Tears can be a great softener.

I recently officiated at a funeral for a young man who had died of AIDS. He was loved deeply by his friends, and many people cried during the service. Towards the end of the funeral, several of his closest friends stood up to sing a song that they had often sung with him. Many of them could barely keep from breaking down as they sang. The pure heartbreak reflected in their faces was so stunning to see; I kept thinking as I watched, that those among them who were actors had probably never given such an honest performance.

Another time, I officiated at the funeral of a young woman who had been brutally murdered. She was married and the mother of a three-year-old baby. I will never forget the look on her husband's face as he sat listening to me in the church. I said to him, "Michael, you will never be the same, we all know that. You have two choices: You will become harder or you will become softer. You will conclude from this that no one, including God, is ever to be trusted again, or you will allow your heartbreak to so soften you—you will allow your tears to so melt the walls that surround your heart—that you will become a man of rare depth and sensitivity."

Then I spoke to the women in the room. "This little boy has lost his mother. This child no longer has a woman's arms around him. Do not let this go uncorrected.

Commit now within your hearts to visit him, to visit his father, to take up the slack as best you can, to become women of mature substance as of this moment. Take this responsibility seriously, that in this one thing, at least, the personal growth brought on by this darkness might be a way in which it is cast out."

Oddly enough, I had to leave that funeral to go across town where I was performing a marriage ceremony. As I gave the service, I noticed a similarity between the eyes of the groom and the eyes of the young man who had just buried his wife. Of course the groom was not grieving, but joyous. What looked the same was the pure unadulterated love in his eyes, with no artificial ingredients placed on top. Just listening, and nakedness, and openness, and love.

Healing is a return to love. Illness and death are often painful lessons in how much we love, but they are lessons nonetheless. Sometimes it takes the knife that emotionally pierces our heart, to pierce the walls that lie in front of it.

One night in Los Angeles, during the meditation period following my lecture, I noticed two of my friends crying in the back of the church. They were in deep sorrow over the impending death of a mutual friend who had AIDS. It hurt me to see them in so much pain. Suffering, I've found, gives you X-ray vision into the suffering of others.

"Can't this burden be lifted?" I asked God. We'd all

seen so much sorrow, so much pain and death from this disease by then. "Isn't this enough? Can't it all be over?"

What occurred to me next was striking. I was reminded of my own "dark night of the soul" almost a decade before. Hadn't I changed from my pain, in deep and ultimately positive ways? If my soul had used that experience as a path to greater awareness of myself, how did I know that these other people weren't doing the same? It isn't my task to judge—to help, in any and every way possible, yes, but not to doubt the ultimate wisdom of all things. The greatest gift we can give to a person in pain is to hold in our own minds the thought that there is a light beyond this darkness. What goes on externally is only the tip of the iceberg in any situation. The lessons, the real changes, the opportunities to grow—these are things the body's eyes can't see. They remain beneath the spiritual water line, but they are there. And they represent a much more vast picture of the soul's journey than what we can see from the perspective of our physical senses. Growth is not always about getting what we think we want. Always, it's about becoming the men and women we have the potential to be. Loving, pure, honest, clear.

A longer life is not necessarily a better life. A healthy life is not determined by physical condition. Life is merely the presence of love, and death is merely its absence. Physical death is not real death at all. We're big enough now to realize that there's life beyond the physi-

cal. As we find that life, we grow into ourselves, as sons
of men and as Sons of God.

8.   DEATH AND REINCARNATION

"There is no death. The Son of God is free."

A Course in Miracles says that birth is not a beginning
but a continuation, and death is not an end but a continuation. Life goes on forever. It always was and always
will be. Physical incarnation is just one form that life can
take.

A Course in Miracles mentions the Great Rays, a
concept also found in other metaphysical teachings. The
Great Rays are lines of energy that emanate from within
each of us, on subtler levels than our physical senses yet
perceive. Our physical senses reflect our current belief
system, and as our belief system expands, so will our
senses. There will come a time when we will physically
perceive the Great Rays. Some people, such as those
who see auras, are already beginning to. Buddha and
Jesus and other enlightened masters are often pictured
with halos around their heads or lines of light radiating
from their hearts.

These lines of light and energy are our life force. The
body is merely a temporary encasement. Because we do
not yet realize this, we think that the death of the body is
the death of the person. It is not. There was a time when
people thought that the earth was flat, and so ships that

reached the horizon were believed to have fallen off the face of the earth. There will come a time when our present perception of death will seem as quaint and ignorant and old-fashioned as that. The spirit does not die when the body dies. Physical death is like taking off a suit of clothes.

To the ego, reality is only what we can perceive physically. But many things that we know to exist cannot be seen with the naked eye—neither atoms nor protons nor viruses nor cells. Scientists are now beginning to recognize a oneness that lies beyond all perceived reality. This oneness is God, and our beingness lies within it.

Physical incarnation is a classroom experience, and souls come to the class to learn what they need to learn. It's much like tuning in to a channel on a television. Let's say we're all tuned to Channel 4. When someone dies, they're no longer on Channel 4, but that doesn't mean they're not broadcasting. They're now on Channel 7 or 8. Cable systems exist regardless of whether or not we have the cable equipment with which to receive them. It is only the arrogance of the ego that would have us believe that what we can't physically perceive must not exist.

People have reported seeing a light exiting through the top of the head of a dying person. Many people have also spoken of their "near-death experiences," where the physical body is let go temporarily. I once met a young woman who had been in a major plane crash. She lost over half the blood in her body and her legs were almost completely severed. In describing her experience to me, she said, "I died and then came back. It felt seductive, very warm, like a wonderful motherly love. But I knew I had a choice. I thought of my father, and I knew my death would be unbearable for him, so I fought and came back.

"I never cry at funerals anymore," she said. "I can cry for the people who are left here, but I know from my experience that the people who died are in a wonderful place."

Once the Great Rays are registered by our physical senses, the body will seem to be a mere shadow in front of our true selves. When we hear that someone has died, it will merely mean that a shadow has been removed. Death will no longer be perceived as the end of a relationship. When Jesus said that Death shall be the last enemy, he meant that it shall be the last thing we perceive as an enemy. The problem is not really death, but what we think death is. We will all die. Some of us will take the 9:30, and some of us will be on the 10:07, but we are all headed out. Accepting a healing of our thoughts about what that means is a cornerstone in our transformation from body to spirit orientation.

Life is like a book that never ends. Chapters close, but not the book itself. The end of one physical incarnation is like the end of a chapter, on some level setting up the beginning of another. I once heard a friend say, "My relationship with my father has only improved since his death."

A Course in Miracles says that communication does not stop with the destruction of the physical body. True communication rests on more than what is said or heard physically. When someone has died, we must speak with them differently than we did before, but in staying open to the possibility of an eternal life force, we direct our minds to develop the capacity for a transphysical conversation.

Letter-writing can help foster such communication. First we write a letter to the person who has died, and then we write another letter back, from them to us. What is the point of such exercises? They expand the mind to accept greater possibilities than the ego normally allows us to consider. People in my grief support groups have often told me that they had had a dream about someone who had died. When the "dead" person had shown up in the dream, the dreamer would say "You can't be here. You're dead." At that point, the person would say, "Oh," and the dream would end. It had been denied permission to continue.

Writing the letters, or having any other kind of conversation or experience that broadens our openness to the possibility of life beyond death, stretches our self-imposed mental boundaries. Our dreams and other emotional experiences then become freed from the bondage of our refusal to believe. Sometimes when someone has died we say, "This isn't happening. It feels unreal. I feel like they're still here." That's because they are. Although the ego voices of the world will say, "It's just your imagination," the truth is that it is death itself that is "just our imagination." The truth as God created it is that death does not exist, and deep in our hearts we know that this is true.

What about reincarnation? The following is from the chapter on reincarnation in the Teacher's Manual of the Course:

> *"In the ultimate sense, reincarnation is impossible. There is no past or future, and the idea of birth into a body has no meaning either once or many times. Reincarnation cannot, then, be true in any real sense. . . . If [the concept] is used to strengthen the recognition of the eternal nature of life, it is helpful indeed. . . . Like many other beliefs, it can be bitterly misused. At least, such misuse offers preoccupation and perhaps pride in the past. At worst, it induces inertia in the present. . . . There is always some risk in seeing the present in terms of the past. There is always some good in any thought which strengthens the idea that life and the body are not the same."*

Technically then, reincarnation doesn't exist in quite the way we think of it simply because there is no linear time. If we have past lives, or future lives, then they're all happening at once. Still, it's helpful to be reminded that we have a life separate from the experience of any one physical lifetime. *A Course in Miracles* has no doctrine.

An advanced student of the Course may or may not believe in reincarnation. The only meaningful question is whether a concept is helpful. We are told to ask our own Internal Teacher for guidance in our thinking about any idea and its use in our lives.

In the enlightened world, we will still drop the body. But death will be experienced very differently. It is written in "The Song of Prayer," an extension of *A Course in Miracles*:

> *"This is what death should be; a quiet choice, made joyfully and with a sense of peace, because the body has been kindly used to help the Son of God along the way he goes to God. We thank the body, then, for all the service it has given us. But we are thankful, too, the need is done to walk the world of limits, and to reach the Christ in hidden form and clearly seen at most in lovely flashes. Now we can behold Him without blinders, in the light that we have learned to look upon again.*
>
> *We call it death, but it is liberty. It does not come in forms that seem to be thrust down in pain upon unwilling flesh, but as a gentle welcome to release. If there has been true healing, this can be the form in which death comes when it is time to rest a while from labor gladly done and gladly ended. Now we go in peace to freer air and gentler climate, where it*

*is not hard to see the gifts we gave were saved for
us. For Christ is clearer now; His vision more
sustained in us; His voice, the word of God,
more certainly our own.*

*This gentle passage to a higher prayer, a kind
forgiveness of the ways of earth, can only be
received with thankfulness."*

I once read of an ancient Japanese religion that cele-
brated when people died, and mourned when they were
born. It was understood that birth meant the forcing of
an infinite spirit into a finite focus, while death meant the
release of all limits and the freedom to live the full range
of possibilities that God in His mercy offers us.

Life is much more than the life of the body; it is an
infinite expanse of energy, a continuum of love in count-
less dimensions, a psychological and spiritual experience
independent of physical form. We have been alive forever. We will be alive forever more. But the life of the
body is an important classroom. It is our opportunity to
deliver the world from Hell. "Dear God, may your will
be done, on earth as it is in Heaven."

CHAPTER 9

Heaven

"Heaven is here. There is nowhere else. Heaven is now. There is no other time."

1. THE DECISION TO BE HAPPY

"Heaven is a decision I must make."

God's will is that we be happy now. In asking that God's will be done, we are instructing our minds to focus on the beauty in life, to see all the reasons to celebrate instead of mourn.

Usually we figure out what we think would make us happy, and then try to make those things happen. But happiness isn't circumstance-dependent. There are people who have every reason in the world to be happy who aren't. There are people with genuine problems who are. The key to happiness is the decision to be happy.

There has been a lot of talk in the last few years about "allowing our feelings." It's an important concept, but one that can be used by the ego for its own purposes. Most of the time, when we hear someone say "feel your feelings," they mean feel the negative ones: "Feel your pain," "feel your anger," "feel your shame." But we need support in feeling our positive feelings just as much as we need support in feeling our negative ones. It is the experience of genuine emotion of any kind that the ego resists. We need support and permission to feel our love, to feel our satisfaction and to feel our happiness.

The ego does hidden battle against happiness. I remember when I was in college, walking around with books of Russian poetry under my arm, cultivating what I felt was a sophisticated, cynical frown worthy of my intellectual prowess. I felt it indicated that I understood the human condition. Ultimately I realized that my cynicism revealed very little understanding of the human condition, because the most important facet of that condition is that we are always at choice. We can always choose to perceive things differently.

There is an old cliché, "You can see the glass half empty, or you can see it half full." You can focus on what's wrong in your life, or you can focus on what's right. But whatever you focus on, you're going to get more of. Creation is an extension of thought. Think lack, and you get lack. Think abundance, and you get more.

"But when I'm going on like everything's great, I'm not being honest with myself," I can hear the voices say. But the negative self is not our honest self; rather, it is the impostor. We need to be in touch with our negative feelings, but only in order to release them and feel the love which lies beneath them.

It's not so difficult to feel positive feelings or think positive thoughts. The problem is that we resist them.

They make us feel guilty. To the ego, there is no greater crime than claiming our natural inheritance. If I'm rich, says the ego, someone else will be poor. If I become successful, someone's feelings might get hurt. Who am I to have it all? I'll be a threat and people won't like me anymore. These are some of the arguments the ego spews into our consciousness. The Course admonishes us to beware the danger of a hidden belief. A hidden belief that many of us hold is that there is something wrong with being too happy.

The ego's religious dogma hasn't helped. Suffering has been glorified. People have focused on the crucifixion more than the resurrection. But crucifixion without the resurrection is a meaningless symbol. Crucifixion is the energy pattern of fear, the manifestation of a closed heart. Resurrection is the reversal of that pattern, brought about by a shift in thought from fear to love.

Look at the crucifixion, says *A Course in Miracles*, but do not dwell upon it. "Blessed are those who have faith who cannot see," says Jesus. It's easy to have faith when things are going well. But there are times in everyone's life when we have to fly on instruments, just like a pilot making a landing in low visibility. He knows the land is there, but he can't see it. He must trust his instruments to navigate for him. And so it is with us, when things aren't what we'd like them to be. We know that life is always in process, and always on its way to greater good. We just can't see that. During those times, we rely on our spiritual radar to navigate for us. We trust there's a happy ending. By our faith, through our trust, we invoke its proof.

Resurrection is actively called forth. It represents the decision to see light in the midst of darkness. In the Talmud, the Jewish book of wisdom, the Jew is told how to behave in the midst of dark times. "During the time of the darkest night," says the Talmud, "act as if the morning has already come."

God provides the answer to every problem the moment it occurs. Time, as we've already seen, is just a thought. It is the physical reflection of our faith or faithlessness. If we think it's going to take time for a wound to heal, it will. If we accept God's will as already accomplished, we experience the healing of all wounds immediately. As cited in the Course, "Only infinite patience produces immediate results." The universe is created to support us in every way. God is constantly expressing His infinite care for us. The only problem is, we don't agree with Him. We don't love ourselves as He loves us, and so we block our experience of the miracles to which we're entitled.

The world has taught us we are less than perfect. In fact, we have been taught that it's arrogant to think we're deserving of total happiness. This is the point where we're stuck. If anything comes into our lives— love, success, happiness—which seems like it would be suited to a "deserving" person, our subconscious mind concludes it can't possibly be for us. And so we sabotage. Few people have wronged us like we've wronged ourselves. No one has snatched the candy away from us like we've thrown it away from ourselves. We have been unable to accept joy because it doesn't match who we think we are.

In contrast to the ego's meager appraisal of our worth, stands truth as God created it. There is no light more bright than the light that shines within us. Whether or not we see that light is irrelevant. It's there because God placed it there.

It is not only our right, but in a way, our responsibility to be happy. God doesn't provide any of us with happiness that is only meant for us alone. When God sends us happiness, he does so in order that we might then stand up more fully in the world on His behalf.

Happiness is a sign that we have accepted God's will. It's a lot easier to frown than to smile. It's easy to be cynical. In fact, it's an excuse for not helping the world. Whenever people say to me, "Marianne, I'm so depressed about world hunger," I say to them, "Do you give five dollars a month to one of the organizations that feed the hungry?" The reason I ask is that I have noticed that people who participate in the solution to problems, don't seem to find themselves as depressed about those problems as do people standing on the sidelines doing nothing. Hope is born of participation in hopeful solutions. We are happy to the extent that we choose to notice and to create the reasons for happiness. Optimism and happiness are the results of spiritual work.

A Course in Miracles states, "Love waits on welcome, not on time." Heaven merely awaits our acceptance. It is not something we'll experience "later." "Later" is just a thought. "Be of good cheer," said Jesus "for I have overcome the world." He realized, and so can we all, that the world has no power before the power of God. It is not real. It is only an illusion. God has created love as the only reality, the only power. And so it is.

2.   OUR CAPACITY FOR BRILLIANCE

"You can stretch out your hand and reach to Heaven."

In the eyes of God, we're all perfect and we have unlimited capacity to express brilliantly. I say unlimited capacity rather than unlimited potential, because potential can be a dangerous concept. We can use it to tyrannize ourselves, to live in the future instead of in the present, to set ourselves up for despair by constantly measuring ourselves against what we think we could be rather than what we are. Until we're perfect masters, it is by definition impossible to live up to our potential. Our potential always remains something we're only capable of living later.

Potential is a concept that can bind us to personal powerlessness. Focus on human potential remains impotent without a focus on human capacity. Capacity is expressed in the present. It is immediate. The key to it lies not in what we have inside of us, but rather in what we are willing to own that we have inside of us. There is no point in waiting until we are perfect in what we do, or enlightened masters, or Ph.D.s in life, before opening ourselves to what we're capable of doing now. Of course, we're not as good today as we'll be tomorrow, but how will we ever get to tomorrow's promise without making some sort of move today? I remember spending years of my life so upset about the life choices I felt I had available, that I never moved. I was paralyzed by all the possibilities. I couldn't figure out which road would lead me to the fulfillment of my "potential"; this glorious neurotic myth that lay always just in front of anything I could manifest now. So I was always too scared to move. And fear, of course, is the great betrayer of Self. The difference between those people "living their potential" and those who don't, is not the amount of potential itself, but the amount of permission they give themselves to live in the present.

We are the adult generation. We have adult bodies, adult responsibilities, and adult careers. What many of us lack is an adult context for our lives, one in which we give ourselves permission to shine, to blossom fully, to show up powerfully in the present without fearing that we're not good enough. Waiting for a powerful future is a way of making sure it never gets here. An adolescent dreams of what will be. An adult takes joy in today.

I once had a therapist who told me that my problem was that I wanted to move directly from point A to point X, Y, and Z. She pointed out that I seemed incapable of moving from point A to point B, of putting one foot in front of another. It's much easier to dream about point Z than to actually move to point B. It's easier to practice our Oscar acceptance speech, than to get up and go to acting class.

We're often afraid to do anything unless we know we can do it extremely well. But we get to Carnegie Hall by practicing. I remember how freeing it was several years ago to read in an interview with Joan Baez that some of Bob Dylan's early songs weren't so wonderful. We have this image of genius springing fully grown out of Zeus's forehead. I once asked someone to lecture for me while I was out of town, and he answered that he felt he couldn't lecture as well as I. "Of course you can't!" I said. "I've been doing it for years! But how will you ever *get* great at it unless you start doing it?" I think the reason people don't have hobbies today as much as they did in past generations, is because we can't bear to do anything we're not fabulous at. Several years ago I started taking piano lessons again, after having played for many years as a child. Chopin, I'm not, but there was so much therapeutic value in just playing. I saw very clearly that you don't have to be a virtuoso at everything you do, in order to be a virtuoso at life. Virtuosity in life means singing out—not necessarily singing well.

Most of us feel on some level like race horses champing at the bit, pressing at the gate, hoping and praying for someone to open the door and let us run out. We feel so much pent up energy, so much locked up talent. We know in our hearts that we were born to do great things, and we have a deep-seated dread of wasting our lives. But the only person who can free us is ourselves. Most of us know that. We realize that the locked door is our own fear. But we have learned by now, that on some level our terror of moving forward is so great that it would take a miracle to free us.

The ego would have us born with great potential, and die with great potential. In between, there is ever-increasing suffering. A miracle frees us to live fully in the present, to release our power and to claim our glory. The Son of God is risen to Heaven when he releases the past, releases the future, and thus releases himself to be who he is today. Hell is what the ego makes of the present. Heaven is another take on the altogether.

3.   *SPIRITUAL PRACTICE*

"An untrained mind can accomplish nothing."

Love takes more than crystals and rainbows, it takes discipline and practice. It's not just a sweet sentiment from a Hallmark card. It is a radical commitment to a different way of being, a mental response to life that is completely at odds with the thinking of the world. Heaven is a conscious choice to defy the ego's voice. The more time we spend with the Holy Spirit, the greater our capacity is to focus on love. *A Course in Miracles* tells us that five minutes spent with Him in the morning (doing the Workbook or any other serious practice of prayer or meditation) guarantees that He will be in charge of our thought forms throughout the day. What that means is that we take responsibility for making what in Alcoholics Anonymous is called "conscious contact" with Him. Just as we go to the gym to build up our physical musculature, so we meditate and pray to build up our mental musculature. The Course says we achieve so little because we have undisciplined minds: we instinctively go into paranoid or judgmental, fearful reactions instead of loving ones. The Course says we are far too indulgent of mind-wandering. Meditation disciplines the mind.

When we meditate, our brains literally emit different brain waves. We receive information at a deeper level than we do during normal waking consciousness. *A Course in Miracles* says that its Workbook is the crux of the Course, because the exercises train our minds to think along the lines the text sets forth. It's not *what* we think that transforms us, but *how* we think. The principles of miracles become "mental habits" in our "problem-solving repertoire."

Spiritual growth is not about becoming more metaphysically complicated, but rather it is about growing simpler, as these very basic principles begin to permeate more and more deeply into our thought system. Meditation is time spent with God in silence and quiet listening. It is the time during which the Holy Spirit has a chance to enter into our minds and perform His divine alchemy. What changes because of this is not just what we do, but who we are.

In the Workbook of *A Course in Miracles*, which is a 365-day set of psychological exercises, we are given a very specific curriculum for relinquishing a thought system based on fear and accepting instead a thought system based on love. Each day, we are given a specific thought to focus on, eyes closed, for a specific amount of time. We're even told in the introduction that we don't have to like the exercises and we might even be hostile to them, but we should just *do* them. Our attitude doesn't affect their efficacy in any way. If I'm lifting weights at the gym, I can either love the experience or hate it, but it doesn't really matter. All that affects my body is whether or not I lift the weights. So it is with meditation. Also, as with physical exercise, the effects of meditation are cumulative. When we go to the gym and work out for an hour, we don't really see any change in our bodies at the end of the hour. If we go every day for thirty days, however, then we do see a change. So it is with meditation. And sometimes, we're not the ones who can see the change as much as others can. We might not even be aware of how much the quality of our energy, the invisible emanations of our minds, affect our environment and the people within it. But others do. And they respond accordingly.

Spiritual practice supports the development of personal power. Spiritually powerful people are not necessarily people who do so much, as they are people around whom things get done. Gandhi caused the British to leave India, but he wasn't a man who ran around a lot. Powerful forces swirled around him. President Kennedy is another example. Legislatively, he achieved relatively little, but he unleashed invisible forces within others that altered the consciousness of at least one American generation. At the highest level of our being, we don't *do* anything. We are at rest when the power of God works through us. Meditation is a profound relaxation. The ego's frantic voice, its vain imaginings, are burned away.

We all have within us a direct radio line to the voice for God. The problem is, the radio is full of static. In our quiet times we spend with God, the static melts away. We learn to hear the small still voice for God. In Heaven, that is the only voice we hear. That is why we are happy there.

4.   *SEEING THE LIGHT*

> *"Child of light, you know not that the light is in you."*

Only the light within us is real. We are not afraid of the dark within ourselves, so much as we are afraid of the light. The dark is familiar. It's what we know. "Yet neither oblivion nor hell is as unacceptable to you as Heaven." The light, the thought that we might indeed be good enough, is such a threat to the ego that it takes out its very big guns to defend against it.

Someone I know remarked to me about a mutual

friend, "He has a mean-spirited soul." "No, he doesn't," I replied. "He has a mean-spirited personality. His soul is one of the brightest I've ever seen. His mean-spiritedness is simply a defense against the light. If he were to let in his light and choose to really express all his love, it would overwhelm his ego. His meanness is his armor, his protection against the light."

Our defense against light is always some form of guilt that we project onto ourselves or others. God can love us infinitely, the universe can support us unendingly, but until we agree with God's kind appraisal of us and the universe's merciful behavior, we will do everything in our power to keep the miracles we're entitled to at bay. Why the self-hatred? As we've already seen, the ego is our mind's endless need to attack itself. And how do we escape this? Through the acceptance of God's will as our own. God's will is that we be happy. God's will is that we forgive ourselves. God's will is that we find our place in Heaven now.

It is not our arrogance but our humility which teaches us that who we are is good enough, and what we have to say is valid. It is our own self-hatred that makes it difficult for us to consistently support and nurture other people, because supporting others amounts to supporting ourselves. When I speak publicly, there is a palpably different feeling between audiences who want me to win, and those who are sitting back signalling, "Oh yeah? *Show* me." The former is a context in which

I am invited to shine, and the latter is one in which I am challenged to shine. Isn't life challenging enough? Is human kindness so lightweight?

When we know that love is an infinite resource—that there is enough abundance of every kind for every one and that only what we give to others we get to keep—then we stop denigrating other people, and start blessing them instead. Several years ago I was living in a house with a teenage girl. One day I came home and she was sitting on her bed with five or six girlfriends, surrounding a poster of Christie Brinkley. As hard as it is to believe this, these girls were struggling to make a case for the fact that Christie Brinkley wasn't really all that beautiful, or if she was, she probably wasn't all that smart. I gently pointed out to them that what was really going on was that each of them wanted very much to look just like her, but were defending against it because they thought it was impossible. "It's okay for you to want to be beautiful, too." I said. "In fact, it's good, and in your own ways you can be. The way to do that is to bless her beauty, praise it, permit it to be so you can permit your own. Christie Brinkley being beautiful doesn't mean that you don't get to be. There's enough beauty to go around. It's just an idea. Anyone can have it. As you bless what she has, you multiply your chances of having it too."

A person who succeeds in any area is only creating more of a possibility for others to do the same. Holding on to the thought of finite resources is a way of holding on to hell.

We must learn to think only divine thoughts. Angels are the thoughts of God, and in Heaven, humans think like angels. Angels light the way. Angels do not begrudge anyone anything, angels do not tear down, angels do not compete, angels do not constrict their hearts, angels do not fear. That's why they sing and that's how they fly. We, of course, are only angels in disguise.

5.   THE END OF THE WORLD

> *"The end of the world is not its destruction, but its translation into Heaven."*

The end of the world as we know it wouldn't be such a horrible thing, if you think of all the ways in which the world is full of pain and suffering. In the "end days," we will not escape the horrors of the world through vehicles that soar into outer space, but through vehicles that soar into inner space. Those vehicles are our healed minds, guided by the Holy Spirit.

What does Heaven look like? Most of us have only had tiny glimpses, but those glimpses were enough to keep us always hoping to go back. The Course says there's an "ancient melody" we all remember, always beckoning, always calling us to return. Heaven is our home. It's where we came from. It's our natural state.

We've all had Heavenly moments on earth, usually at our mother's breast or at someone else's. There is a feeling of inner peace that comes from total relinquishment of judgment. We don't feel the need to change others, and we don't feel the need to be different than we are. We can see, for whatever reason, the total beauty of another person, and we feel that they can see the beauty in us as well.

The world sees the special relationship, whether romantic or otherwise, as the only valid context for such an experience. That is our primary neurosis, our most painful delusion. We keep looking to the body for love, but it is not there. We embark upon an endless search for what we cannot find—one person, one circumstance that holds the key to Heaven. But Heaven is within us. It has nothing ultimately to do with the thoughts of someone else, and everything to do with what we choose to think ourselves, not just about one person, but about all people. So forgiveness of mankind, of everyone in every circumstance, is our ticket to Heaven, our only way home.

Our goal is God. Nothing short of that goal will bring us joy. And it is joy to which we are entitled. Although we're relatively aware of the transformative power of pain, we know very little about the transformative power of joy because we know so little about joy at all.

Talk of joy is not simplistic. No one is saying that it's easy; we're just affirming that it's our goal. As we've already seen, there is no getting to Heaven without acknowledging hell—not its ultimate reality, but its reality for us while we remain in this illusion. This illusion is very powerful indeed. *A Course in Miracles* is not proposing emotional denial and suppression of darkness as a way to light. It is a psychotherapeutic process by which darkness is brought to light—not the other way around. In the enlightened world, psychotherapy, guided by the Holy Spirit, will certainly have a place. According to the Course, "No one can escape from illusions unless he looks at them, for not looking is the way they are protected." The way to Heaven is fraught with demons on the side of the road, just as the fairy tale castle is surrounded by dragons.

A Course in Miracles says, "What is healing but the removal of all that stands in the way of knowledge? How else can one dispel illusions except by looking at them directly, without protecting them?" The work toward enlightenment often entails a painful and not very pretty arousal of the worst of which we're capable, made plain to both ourselves and others, in order that we might consciously choose to release our personal darkness. But without a commitment to light, a conscious intent to go for Heaven, we remain enamored of darkness, too tempted by its complexities.

The temptation to analyze darkness as a way to light is illustrated in some traditional psychotherapeutic models. When used by the ego, psychotherapy is a tool for endless ego investigation: assignment of blame and focus on the past. When used by the Holy Spirit, it is a search for light. It is a sacred interaction in which two people together, consciously or unconsciously, invite the Holy Spirit to enter into their relationship, and to transform painful perceptions into loving knowledge. The only reason we all need therapy so much is because we've lost an essential connection to the meaning of friendship. Real relationship of any kind is a form of psychotherapy, as is true religion. The Holy Spirit's psychotherapists, professional or otherwise, ask only to accept the Atonement for themselves, that their own healed perceptions might help enlighten others.

In the world to come, couples will use psychotherapy more and more frequently, not as crisis counseling, but as maintenance procedure. There was a time when most people saw therapy as something you did only if you were "crazy." Now we see it as a valuable tool for staying sane. So it is that couples will come to see the value in a constant and consistent, formal evaluation of their thoughts and feelings as they walk two by two into the arms of God.

Just outside of Heaven's gate, there's a lot of action—all within an illusion, of course, but an illusion that must be transformed from within. The only meaning of any event within the world of form is that it stimulates within us an impulse to reach for the gate, or turn our back on Heaven. As we stand before the gate, uncertain of which way to go, impelled to love and yet so trained to fear, we need to realize the sacred responsibility that has been placed in our hands. "And so you walk toward Heaven or toward hell, but not alone." We choose for everyone, for many years to come.

The decisions we make today, individually and collectively, will determine whether the planet goes to hell or goes to Heaven. One thing, however, is sure: we are the transitional generation. The critical choices lie in our hands. Future generations will know who we were. They will think of us often. They will curse us, or they will bless us.

6.   HEAVEN'S GATE

"Think not the way to Heaven's gate is difficult at all."

We are poised at Heaven's gate. In our minds, we left there millions of years ago. Today we are returning home.

We are a Prodigal Son generation. We left home and now there's an excitement in the air because we're back. We did everything to violate love, of ourselves and others, before a life of wholesomeness began to attract us. That's not our shame but our strength. There are certain doors we don't have to go through because a false moralism said not to, but because we opened them already and we know they lead nowhere. Oddly enough, this gives us a kind of moral authority. We speak from experience. We've done the dark side. We're ready to move on. We're attracted to the light. When Bhagwan Shree

Rajneesh was asked by his disciples, "Why does it say in Scripture, 'God loves a sinner'?" his answer was, "They tend to be more interesting people."

We're an interesting generation; we just don't see that about ourselves. When I first realized what a decisive time this is, that the decisions made on this planet in the next twenty years will determine whether or not mankind survives much longer, I was afraid for the world. The fate of the world is left up to us? Not us, I thought. Anyone but us. We're spoiled brats, morally bankrupt. But when I looked more closely, what I saw surprised me. We're not bad. We're wounded. And our wounds are simply our opportunities to heal.

Outside Heaven's gate, healing is the buzzword, and it is shaping our desires. There is a holy return in the air today, despite the pain, despite the conflicts. Enough people have taken on its mandate, consciously or unconsciously, to have already caused the feeling of a cautious excitement, a hope for Heaven. In every area, there are at least vague intimations of greater responsibilities.

Before we awaken, the Holy Spirit transforms our bitter dreams into happy ones. Here are some reflections on a few happy dreams that could possibly bring the whole world a little closer to Heaven.

There has to be a mass, collective forgiveness of what went before in order for our culture to have a chance to heal itself and begin again. Some of the best and the brightest that America has to offer are dropping through the cracks because they can't shake their pasts. How sad for America that anyone who has had too much sex or drugs in their past, for instance, is too scared to enter politics for fear of being crucified for their personal histories. The important thing about our past is not what happened, but what we have done with what happened. Anything can contribute to our being a more compassionate person now, if we choose.

The meaningful question is never what we did yesterday, but what we have learned from it and are doing today. No one can counsel a recovering alcoholic like another recovering person, who has been on the road to recovery longer. No one can counsel a person in grief like someone who has grieved. No one can help with anything like someone who has been through the pain themselves.

I never had much interest in Richard Nixon until I saw him on television a few years after he left the White House. This man, I thought, has suffered complete humiliation, which he can blame on no one but himself. The only way that any person could survive such a crushing experience would be if he got on his knees and threw himself into the arms of God. Watching him on the screen, I felt that he had done just that. I saw a softness in his face that we had never seen before. *Now* this man is interesting, I said to myself. He seems to have tasted the fires of purification. Now he has more to offer us than ever. Now I would trust him to speak to me from a more genuine place.

Just outside the gate, we're never afraid to apologize. How wonderful it would be for America if we were to make amends, in our hearts and to the world, for the violation of our own most sacred principles in dealing with nations such as Vietnam. We are a great country, and like all nations, we have made our mistakes. Our greatness lies not in our military might but in our holding to sacred, internal truths. A big nation, like a big individual, admits when it has made mistakes, atones for its errors, and asks God and man for a chance to begin again. This would not make us look weak to the rest of the world. It would make us look humble and honest, two traits without which there is not greatness.

And wouldn't it be wonderful—Abraham Lincoln paved the way—if we could just make one huge, simple apology to all black Americans? "On behalf of our ancestors, we apologize for bringing you here as slaves from your native home. We recognize the pain that this terrible violation has caused generations of good people. Please forgive us. Let us begin again." And then, the least we can do is build a lasting memorial to the American slaves. White Americans have more of an internal need to do this than blacks. Afro-Americans will find it much easier to forgive us when we have asked for forgiveness. All of these things, of course, apply as well to the American Indians. Until this Atonement, there will be little room for a miraculous healing of our racial tensions.

The parades for our soldiers coming home from the Persian Gulf conflict, for me, represented in part an attempt to rectify our harsh treatment of Vietnam veterans. I just wish there were parades for our teachers, our scientists and our other national treasures.

Speaking of national treasures, children are our most important resources. For a fraction of the cost of keeping one criminal in jail for a year, we could provide a child from an underprivileged background a plethora of personal and educational opportunities that would occlude the propensity to hopeless despair. The temptation to experience drugs, delinquency and other paths to a criminal behavior would then be greatly diminished. There is no amount of money, time or energy too great to spend on our children. They are our angels, our future. In failing them, we are failing ourselves.

Just outside the gate, there is so much to do, as we allow the motivation for a transformed world to energize our souls and make manifest our convictions. We must have faith in God and faith in ourselves. Whatever He wills, He can let us know, and whatever He wants done, He can show us how to do it. In every community, there is work to be done. In every nation, there are wounds to heal. In every heart, there is the power to do it.

7.   CHRISTMAS

> *"The sign of Christmas is a star, a light in the darkness."*

Christmas is a symbol of change. The meaning of Christmas is the birth of a new self, mothered by our humanness and fathered by God. Mary symbolizes the feminine within us all, who is impregnated by spirit. Her function is to say yes, I will, I receive, I will not abort this process, I accept with humility my holy function. The child born from this mystical conception is the Christ within us all.

The angels awakened Mary in the middle of the night and told her to meet them on the roof. "The middle of the night" symbolizes our darkness, our confusion, our despair. "Come onto the roof" means turn off the television, sober up, read better books, meditate, and pray. The angels are the thoughts of God. We can only hear them in a pure mental atmosphere.

Most of us have heard the angels beckon us to the rooftop already. Otherwise, we would not be reading books like this one. What happens at this point is that we are given the opportunity, the challenge, to accept God's spirit, to allow His seed into our mystical body. We shall be His safety and protection. We shall, if we agree to, allow our hearts to be a womb for the Christ child, a haven in which He can grow in fullness and prepare for earthly birth. God has chosen that His Son be born through each of us.

"There is no room here," said the innkeeper to Joseph. The "inn" is our intellect. There is little if any room there for the things of spirit. But that doesn't matter because God doesn't need it. All he needs is a little space in the manger, just a little willingness on our part in order for Him to be born on earth. There, "surrounded by animals," at one with our natural human self, we give birth to the One who rules the universe.

Shepherds in the field see the "star of Christmas" before anyone else. Shepherds are those who tend the flocks, who care, who protect and heal the children of the earth. Of course they see the sign of hope first, because they are the ones providing it. They have made of their lives fertile ground of miracles. They see the star and they follow the star. They are led to the scene of Jesus in the arms of man.

And worldly kings gather to pay homage to Him. That is because the power of the world is nothing before the power of innocence. The lion lies down with the lamb; our strength is in harmony with our innocence. Our gentleness and our power are not at odds.

"Long lay the world in sin and error pining, till He appeared and the soul felt its worth," goes the Christmas carol. With the birth of Christ, not just once a year but in every moment, we allow ourselves to take on the mantle of divine Sonship, to be more than we were the moment before. We expand our self-awareness and self-identity. The son of man recognizes himself, and in so doing becomes the Son of God.

And thus is the world redeemed, brought back, healed and made whole. The dream of death is over when we receive the vision of real life. Jesus in our hearts is merely the truth that is etched upon it, the "alpha and the omega," where we began and where we will return to. Even if he takes another name, even if he takes another face, He is in essence the truth of who we are. Our joined lives form the mystical body of Christ. To reclaim our place within this body is to return home. We once again find the right relationship to God, to each other, and to ourselves.

8.   *EASTER*

> *"The resurrection's whole compelling power lies in the fact it represents what you want to be."*

Christmas and Easter are attitudinal bookends for an enlightened worldview. With an enlightened view of Christmas, we understand that it is within our power, through God, to give birth to a divine Self. With an enlightened view of Easter, we understand that this Self is the power of the universe, before which death itself has no real power.

Resurrection is the symbol of joy. It is the great "aha!"—the sign of total understanding that we are not at the effect of lovelessness, in ourselves and others. The acceptance of the resurrection is the realization of the fact that we need wait no longer to see ourselves as healed and whole.

I was sitting around talking with my girlfriend Barbara. She had recently experienced a kind of emotional triple-header: her father lay dying, she broke up with a boyfriend of seven years, and then she fell into a rather passionate liaison with a classic "Peter Pan." As we discussed the principles of resurrection and our desire for Heaven, she remarked to me, "I guess I just have to trust that God has a plan, and that things will get better when they're supposed to."

In a desire to understand the principles of *A Course in Miracles* as deeply as possible, I pointed out to her that, theoretically, since there is no time, this has nothing to do with God saving us "later." The message of resurrection is that the crucifixion never occurred, except in our minds. Christ-consciousness is not that the wounds of her father's death will heal, or that her break-up with the boyfriend would grow more comfortable in time, or that her affair would one day turn into a friendship. Christ-consciousness is the understanding that Heaven is here now: her father will not die when he dies, the change of form in the long-term relationship means absolutely nothing because the love itself is changeless, and Peter Pan's departure means nothing because the bond that unites them is eternal. Her sadness rests not on fact, but on fiction. It is her interpretation of events, and the events themselves, that keeps her heart in chains. Heaven is the transformation of these events within her mind. The physical world then follows. The resurrection is our awakening from the dream, our return to right-mindedness, and thus our deliverance from hell.

And so she gladdened. Barbara and I laughed like little children as we allowed ourselves to scan our lives, the relationships, the circumstances, the events that make up our crosses to bear. We recognized how avidly we drill the nails into our own hands and feet, holding on to earthly interpretation of things when a choice to do otherwise would release us and make us happy. We prayed for a more consistent ability to remember that only love is real. We saw, if even for a few minutes, the needlessness of our despair. We saw in that time a glimpse of Heaven and we prayed for the ability to experience more of it.

From *A Course in Miracles*:

> "The journey to the cross should be the last 'useless journey.' Do not dwell upon it, but dismiss it as accomplished. If you can accept it as your own last useless journey, you are also free to join my resurrection. Until you do so, your life is indeed wasted. It merely re-enacts the separation, the loss of power, the futile attempts of the ego at reparation, and finally the crucifixion of the body, or death. Such repetitions are endless until they are voluntarily given up. Do not make the pathetic error of "clinging to the old rugged cross." The only message of the crucifixion is that you can overcome the cross. Until then you are free to crucify yourself as often as you choose. This is not the gospel I intended to offer you. We have another journey to undertake, and if you will read these lessons carefully they will help prepare you to undertake it."

At the end of the Workbook, we are told "This course is a beginning, not an end." A spiritual path is not home; it is a road home. Home is within us, and every moment we are choosing to rest there, or to fight the experience. Our real terror, says the Course, is of redemption.

But there is within us One who knows the truth, who has been given by God the job of outwitting our ego, outsmarting our self-hatred. The Christ does not attack our ego; He transcends it. And He is within us every moment, in every circumstance. He is to our left and to our right, before us and behind us, above us and beneath us. He responds fully to our slightest invitation.

With our prayers we invite Him in, He who is already there. With prayer, we speak to God. With miracles, He responds. The endless chain of communication between loved and lover, between God and man, is the most beautiful song, the sweetest poem. It is the highest art and the most passionate love.

> *Dear God,*
>
> *I give this day to you, the fruit of my labor and the desires of my heart. In your hands I place all questions, on your shoulders I place all burdens. I pray for my brothers and for myself. May we return to love. May our minds be healed. May we all be blessed. May we find our way home, from the pain to peace, from fear to love, from hell to Heaven.*

Thy Kingdom come, thy will be done, on earth as it is in Heaven.

For Thine is the Kingdom, and the Power, and the Glory.

Forever and ever.

Amen.

ABOUT THE AUTHOR

Marianne Williamson is an internationally acclaimed author and lecturer. Six of her ten published books have been *New York Times* bestsellers. These include *A Return to Love, The Age of Miracles, Everyday Grace, A Woman's Worth, Illuminata, Healing the Soul of America,* and *The Gift of Change.* Marianne's *A Course in Weight Loss: 21 Spiritual Lessons for Surrendering Your Weight Forever* was selected by Oprah to be one of her Favorite Things in 2010. She has been a popular guest on television programs such as *The Oprah Winfrey Show, Larry King Live, Good Morning America,* and *Charlie Rose.* In December 2006, a *Newsweek* magazine poll named Marianne Williamson one of the fifty most influential baby boomers. According to *TIME* magazine, "Yoga, the Cabala and Marianne Williamson have been taken up by those seeking a relationship with God that is not strictly tethered to Christianity." Visit her website at www.marianne.com.

Explore Other
— *Marianne Williamson Classics* —

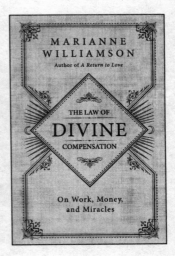

HarperOne
An Imprint of HarperCollinsPublishers